Opinion as Fact
-essays and articles-
by Harding McFadden

Also by Harding McFadden:
The Children's War (with Chester Haas)
The Great First Impressions Trip
The Judas Hymn
Making Monsters (forthcoming)

table of contents:

Introduction

Which Me am I today?

Am I the angry young man (trapped in a middle aged man's body), shouting at the sky and asking why people can never seem to learn anything?

Am I the calm, happy husband and father, feeling blessed by his circumstance?

Am I the optimist, seeing the silver lining, and ready to help anyone at the drop of a hat?

Am I the bitter loner, cursing the stupid, and more than willing to let them drown in the accumulated filth of their own perpetual stupidity?

In truth, I don't know.

The short essays collected here are snapshots of where I was at any particular when and where. They boil down my frustrations, hopes, and headaches into edible bits of vim or vitriol. In truth, as each day passes, I'm both more and less of who I was when I wrote any of these words. Catch me on a good day, when I've managed to avoid the news (or what passes for it), and haven't learned of the passing of a loved one, and I'm all roses and rainbows. Catch me on a bad day, when the baying of Leftist monsters can be clearly heard just outside the door, and I'm of a darker worldview.

I'd like to think that in general I'm a fairly optimistic fella. I've got a spectacular wife, and two incomparable kids to help me see the silver lining, and to hell with the cloud. But there's a part of me, always seeming to be seething just beneath the surface, who sees the grit and grime that seems to be glorified by this broken world. The one who skirts the thin line between righteous anger and self-righteous fury. These days, I just try to avoid the news altogether.

So, here, now, I present to you small glimpses of me as I was, and am, and will be again. The revolving kaleidoscope of ever growing mentality, for better or worse, worts and all. I hope you enjoy it.

-H.G.M. 4/14/22

<u>Choose Your Propaganda</u>
(*The Libertarian Enterprise* July 29, 2018)

All education is propaganda. Let's start there.

The purpose of public education is to indoctrinate children into the kinds of mindset that are most socially acceptable. Regardless of the society or the times, education (or the distinct lack thereof) has been, and always will be, for the sake of shaping citizens or subjects that will adhere to societal norms. This is exactly why public schools, as well as more than a few private ones, preach socialism to their students, casting capitalists and other right-leaning persons as evil. Is it any wonder why so many of these kids look at the Cold War and see the West as aggressors, doing their best to bring down the noble Communists, for their own selfish gains? Is it any wonder why those same misguided, brainwashed kids see the Bill of Rights as nothing more than a leash put around the proletariats' necks by a bunch of slave owning racist dictators? We have allowed this to happen, by standing back and letting others raise our children, for eight hours a day, five days a week. The shame is on each of us, and our parents, and anyone else who knew that they could do better, but that doing better was going to require work, and there's already too much of that.

It has been a long time since I was in school, but given what I've heard from nieces and nephews that are still confined there, I can come to the steady conclusion that little has changed, other than the technology involved. I was informed by one such niece that beginning with the next school year, students will not even be receiving textbooks, all scholarly work being done on computer screens. Okay, I get it: no books means no lost books, vandalized books, etc., but what it also does is not give the parents a chance to see what their kids are learning. I remember a movie that I was made to watch in grade school, which told us that it would be good if we were to turn our parents in, should we see them doing anything not good for the collective whole. We were brought in to watch this thing in a dark room, where we sat on the floor, like we were hiding some secret shame. It wasn't until years later that I thought back on it, and saw how shady it was. Telling us all that we were to be part of the thought police, spying on our parents and siblings, for their own good. These things don't even have to be hidden in dark rooms now, however, as we have given free range to the State to remove accountability from the curriculum, taking whatever the teachers and principles say at face value, and not caring what our kids are up to, as long as it doesn't mean our getting called in for a conference. "Just go along with the herd, honey, Mommy and Daddy can't take the time to care right now..."

And what kind of education are they getting? As more than one person has said over the past few years, *Children are taught to take tests.* Though try as I might, I cannot fault the teachers for this. It has become the way that it is. If you want to keep your job, you teach the kids to do well on standardized tests, to disregard what doesn't matter on paper, and to just perform like a good little worker bee. With all of the attention put on looking good, regardless of the styrofoam-brained victims being chucked from the machine, is it any wonder why so many teachers have become lackluster, living week to week, just waiting until they can cash out and do something worthwhile again?

So, all of this ranting, and where am I going with this? There is another way.

I have the pleasure of homeschooling my daughters. Through a mix of textbooks, internet, and conversation, I have seen my kids' minds grow by leaps and bounds, and when there is something in a curriculum that I figure is crap, I'll go through it, and temper it with alternative opinions, if not longwinded speeches about just why the writer of a particular article or book is full of bologna. My wife and I, and God only knows how many

8

other millions of parents, have taken the reigns from faceless bureaucrats, and are raising our kids, our way, for good or bad, and instilling in them our values, our beliefs, our propaganda. Because, as I said at the outset, all education is propaganda. So wouldn't you rather program your kids in a way that you find morally responsible, rather than leaving that task for the socialists that want nothing more than to make little Communists out of your kids?

*2022 update: As of this writing, the number of families homeschooling their children has nearly tripled since mid-2019.

The Fox Realization
(The Libertarian Enterprise August 12, 2018)

I'm not a hunter. It's not that I have some moral objection to hunting. That's not it at all. It's mostly because I prefer hamburgers to steak, don't like venison, and prefer animals to most people. Don't misunderstand: I'm not one of those amoral freaks who'd rather see a landfill overflowing with the corpses of their fellow humans than see one trophy head mounted on someone's den wall. I just don't have the heart for it. Makes me kind of a rarity where I live, let me tell you.

So when I tell you that I killed a fox a few months back, that it was a conscious decision, and that I stand by it, I want you to understand what this act meant to me. And why it reminded me so fully just why I'm not, and can never be, a pacifist.

A few of my in-laws raise chickens. As someone who can't get over the texture of eggs to even begin to appreciate the taste, I don't get the whole chicken thing, but to each their own. Over a period of days, they'd been infiltrated a few times by a fox who'd get into their yard, at their chickens, and away with his catch with no one the wiser until the next morning.

So, one day, while visiting their house, my sister-in-law looks out a window and sees the offending chicken thief skulking his way through their yard on his way to another prize. For some reason that I still can't explain, I offered to drop the little bugger. In the drop of a hat, I was outside, my brother-in-law's rifle in hand, sighting in on the thing. It saw me and started making a slow beeline for me.

Now I've been told that when wild animals start coming toward you that it's a better than average chance that they're rabid and just giddy at the chance to pass it on. I'm not a smart man, so I'm not at all sure if this is true or not. All I know is that as I gawked down the sights at the thing, it trudged toward me, intent on making my acquaintance.

So, I sighted in on the thing, and once the shakes had passed, I shot it, killed it, and went back inside.

The feelings that tried to overwhelm me then are embarrassing to admit—the shakes and slight nausea—but after all it was the first time I'd ever killed something. Something that had until then done me no personal wrong, but had inflicted financial problems on kin, with the ever-present possibility of biting one of the children that either live in or visit their house. So, for better or worse, it had to go, so go it went.

Understand that I took no inherent joy in the killing of that fox. It may have briefly awakened an apparently natural bloodlust in me that had me looking into local hunting seasons, what I could kill, and how many, but that eventually passed as well, and I can hope that I will never be in a position to take a life again.

Which I suppose gets me to the point. I have no inherent inclination to shoot another human being. It is my sincere hope, as well as my prayer to God, that I am never in a position to do so. But, likewise, if I ever find myself up against it, in a position where the lives of myself or another innocent person are at stake, I hope to God that I have the courage to do what's necessary.

Because of where I live, and the people that I interact with, I am surrounded by pacifists. So, again, as a non-agressionist, I stand out in these little social circles. Like them, I don't go out looking for trouble. In fact, if I suspect a place of being somewhere trouble might start, I avoid it unless left with no other choice. But, unlike them, I am not willing—or, indeed, *able*—to allow myself or someone else to die when to do otherwise is possible.

I have random conversations with my kids about good deaths, mostly in regard to books and movies. In most cases, I use two examples: 1.) Spock at the end of *The Wrath of Khan*; and 2.) literally the entire cast of Meredith's brilliant and criminally out-of-print *We All Died at Breakaway Station*. As with so much, I can sum it up Biblically: "Greater love hath no man than this, that a man lay down his life for his friends. (John 15:13)" (A special thanks to Dean Koontz for introducing me to that one in his *Watchers*, which I read decades before my spiritual awakening.)

See, I do feel that there are things greater than oneself. Without something more important than you, why bother? Completely self-centered folks are generally jerks, and really why give them the time of day? There's plenty of nice people out there, without having to deal with the wankers.

I look at my kids, each one a miracle and a gift for some good deed that I, for the life of me, can't remember. I look at them, and know that their secured existence is more important than anything I'll ever do for myself. If I have to die so that they might live, then so be it. I'll go to the hereafter with arms open and a grin on my face, knowing that I went out giving them more time.

And that's why I can't ever be a pacifist. It's why I can't ever look at the world and say, "There's nothing that would ever make me hurt another human being, or take their life." I think it was Charles Askins who said, "Some people just need to be shot." It is because of those people, the ones who need to be shot—the pedophiles, rapists, and casually violent monsters that contemporary society seems hellbent on not just defending, but actually *excusing*—that I cannot be a pacifist. Because there's literally nothing that I wouldn't do to keep my children safe, up to and including the laying down of my life or the lives of those that would do harm to the ones that I love most.

I didn't kill that fox a few months ago because I enjoyed it. I did it because it was something that needed to be done, and I was in a position to do it. Likewise, though I hope to never have to hurt or remove the life from another human being, I will not shy from doing so. Because some folks need to go, and it's left to the rest of us to see them on their way.

*2022 update: Still not a pacifist.

Why Do You Feel?

(*The Libertarian Enterprise* August 19, 2018)

Like most things in my life, I can trace my problems with beliefs back to Robert Heinlein. Y'see, when I was just an impressionable kid I started reading REH's books, beginning with *Starship Troopers*. It was, is, and in all likelihood will forever be my favorite book (unless one of my kids writes something, dedicates it to Dear Ol' Dad, [sorry Bob], and becomes instantly the greatest book ever written).

I remember ripping my way through it the first time in a sitting, falling into the narrative in a way that I'd never have thought possible. True there was a lot in there that I was just too young to fully grasp, and things that on later readings burned my butt but good. Heck, I was nearly an adult before I could go through it without gritting my teeth every few pages. It entertained me. Confronted me. But, most importantly, it made me question.

I was forced to ask myself why I felt the way that I did about things. And this is something that I ask every person who ever had a thought in their head. Why do you feel the way that you do? What is the foundation of your most strongly held beliefs? Do they hold up under scrutiny?

You see, it has come to me that most people that I know feel the way that they do about things because their parents, or friends, or mentors, have told them that they should, and they just never question it. Their opinions may as well have been handed down by God. The only problem with that, is that most of what they feel wasn't handed down by

God, but by man, and man is synonymous with failable.

I am an opinionated person. Anyone who knows me can readily attest that I feel things. In most cases not very strongly. If I'm not ready to fight over something, I generally couldn't care about it. In other cases I feel with a fanaticism that can be publicly embarrassing. Religion, politics, and red-headed women, right?

What Heinlein did for me, and which I could never repay no matter that I should live to be 1,000, was make me question.

As a teenager I was an atheist. An angry one at that. I hated God (which is kinda funny: hating something that I didn't even believe existed, but I digress), religion, religious people regardless of faith. It wasn't until much later that I asked myself why, and started looking heavily into faith, belief, higher powers, and saw that my hate was misplaced. Heck, my arguments lost their footing upon closer inspection, eventually crumbling away when I saw so many overlapping theories between Creation and evolutionary sciences. On the one hand we have "Let there be light;" on the other the Big Bang. In another case we have Eve made from Adam's rib; on the other we have single-celled organisms asexually reproducing. The list goes on and on, but you get my point.

Likewise I was forced to ask myself why I was the way I was politically. I was raised a conservative, with a strong distrust, if not outright dislike, of left-leaning persons (this last never left, as life has shown me more times than I can count that the further left-leaning the ideology, the most the holder of said ideology wants to own the lives, liberties, and pursuits of those surfs they deem beneath them). I never questioned why. Until I was about sixteen or so, and was given copies of L. Neil Smith's *The Probability Broach,* and Dr. Victor Koman's *The Jehovah Contract.* After that I was screwed. And any hope of peaceful nights were abandoned by family and friends who just wanted me to shut up and stop seeing political arguments everywhere.

The problem was that I wasn't just seeing them everywhere. They were there. Like they've always been there. I was just too young to handle the information in a mature way. So the smallest things could set me off on rants that would leave me red-faced and raw. It didn't matter where I was, if there was a fight to be had I had it. No matter who with. For those difficult years between when politics was discovered and rationality was embraced, I'd like to offer a blanket apology to anyone who stumbled across me. My bad.

So now I ask you: why do you feel the way you do? Whatever your loves and hates, why are they there? Are the words coming out of your mouth your own, or are you acting as the voice box by proxy of someone who knew you in your formative years? Are you really what you think you are, or is the real you waiting in the wings, afraid to show their face for fear of confrontation?

My advice? Look at yourself, at what you know to be true, and ask yourself why? Are you a liberal, conservative, Libertarian, Communist? Are you anti-gun, or were you just never given the choice? Are you a Socialist because someone told you that you were owed something earned by someone else, or because you don't want to earn your own keep? Don't be an extension of someone else, because they might not be worth it. Be yourself, know who you are, and embrace it, but never forget to ask why?

Statement of Intent

(The Libertarian Enterprise, August 26, 2018)

History is very important. Not just to me, but to the world in general, showing us where we've been, how we got there, and who took us there. It shows our struggles, our victories, and our failures. It shows us at what point our ancestors looked at the shape of things around them and declared, "No more!" It is important. Which is why what's being shown to contemporary students makes me so angry.

First of all, our children are shown that those that came before were all monsters, unworthy, unless they fall into something that modern liberal thinking can shape into a creature that sycophants can rally behind. Forget the great and awe-inspiring deeds that the founding fathers and their revolutionary contemporaries pulled off, against all odds, against an enemy that by all rights should have shrugged them off like irritating gnats. Why should we remember Washington, Jefferson, or any of their lot as anything other than miserable slave owners? Why see them as the mammoth figures and symbols that they rightly were for two solid centuries? Why look up to some ideal like they embodied when we can look down to the ever more idealized Lenin or Stalin, who were just looking out for the little guy, anyway? Wait, Stalin did *what* to people? Che Guevara was responsible for what? Can't be, they were left-leaning heroes, enemies of the hated west. Plus, if we had to see them as evil, we'd lose half the faces on our T-shirts.

The history being taught in schools today is a sad wash of what has gone before, showing things that matter as little as possible, while emphasizing the failings of great people to the point that they are demonized more than humanized. Early European settlements are shown as nothing more than rapists of the American Indians, thieves and butchers. The heroes of the Revolution are all slave-holding racists (even the ones that weren't). The south fought and killed and died for the sole purpose of holding onto those same slaves. When all was said and done, the only nation more evil than the United States was Nazi Germany; Japan and Italy were just misunderstood, and don't even bring up the Russians and what they were doing before, during, and after the war.

Make no mistake: this is what is being taught to our kids. The shame that comes from being a citizen of the greatest country in the world. Why? Because if you're ashamed of those that came before you, of what they were and what they stood for, then you won't stand against when the evil that they pushed back comes knocking at your door.

So, just in case there's anyone reading this who can't quite grasp which side I come down on, let me be absolutely clear. Communism, Naziism, socialism, group/gang mentality, and the idea that someone owes you something of what they've earned, are Evil ideas (notice the capital "E"), and those that propose them to you are Evil people. It isn't that all those failed attempts at true Communism were wrong because they weren't pure enough. It was wrong, and failed, because Communism is wrong. The same goes for socialism. Likewise the gang mentality, and the idea that someone else owes *you* part of what *they* earned.

This all being the case, I do hereby state my intent to teach those that follow me not the sanitized, politically corrected hate-speech that passes for history in contemporary America.   I will not tell my children that "It was all about slavery" when they ask me why the Civil War was fought.   I will not emphasize the failings of our greatest leaders when asked who they were. I will not promote the idea that soviet Russia, or Cuba, or any of the world's other dictatorial societies are not wrong, but misunderstood, or misguided. Because these things are important.

It is important that those that follow us know what the founders stood for. That the Confederates were not just racists. That the Allies were not the bad guys. They need to understand that there are areas of history that are black and white, that there were good guys and bad guys, and that America wasn't always the aggressor. They need to know that the heroification of Jimmy Carter, Bill Clinton, LBJ, Barry Obama and the lot is so much bunk. They need to understand that JFK did not walk on water, and that it was not a right wing extremist that assassinated him, but one of the left. They need a firmer grasp of history than I had until I was an adult, because if they don't know what happened, how can they know what to fight for?

<u>Bothered?</u>
(2018)

Does it seem to anyone else that the world is made up of two kinds of folks: those who aren't bothered by much of anything, who let words roll off their backs like the hot air that they are; and those who are offended by literally everything, no matter how innocently those things might be stated? Yet, it's always this letter, overly sensitive minority who get their way.   Who shout and shout and shout until those of us who just don't really give two shakes what they have to say are so bogged down in the nicety that is generally in us that we actually clam up, rather than unintentionally offending those sensitives.

I saw a bumper sticker recently that said something like, "I'd care more about what offends you, if only there was something that didn't." Wow, right?   Profound statements splayed across a bumper. Who'd've thunk it?

Because the problem isn't that we are terribly offensive.   It's that these others, these tender wittle kiddies that get all bunched up at the slightest thing, are grasping at relevance.   They see statues to heroes and get angry. They see a Confederate flag and see red. They are presented with something that doesn't fit perfectly into their milquetoast view of life, and they become the bull in the china shop. Because it doesn't matter if they offend us. We don't matter as much as they do. They're superior to us; better than. In the world of equal animals, some are more equal than others, and it is they.

As far as I can see it, there's only one way to help them get over their aversion to individuality: hit them with it even more.

Don't get me wrong, I'm not advocating cornering the spineless little hive-minded weasels and shouting in their pasty faces until they cry, and run home to the basement that they live in, rent free, at mommy and daddy's house. Not at all. Nor am I advocating being intentionally grotesque while in public, as I truly do hold to the old adage that there are things inappropriate to talk about in certain company.

What I am advocating is to not curb yourself. Don't not talk about something just because it *might* upset someone sitting around you. Because, guess what: if you are with a group of folks, and you don't say something that offends at least one of them, then you're doing nothing but adding to the white noise of the environment. You might as well take up practicing bird calls in public, which would at least make you more memorable that the lump sitting next to you that coaches his verbiage in PC rhetoric so intensely that he takes two hundred words to say something for which five would suffice.

If someone asks you: what do you think of the state of politics or religion in America today, don't look at it as a trap that you'll fall into regardless of how you respond. Nope, at that point, it is your responsibility as a warmblooded, opinion holding human being to throw a verbal grande into the conversation, and see where the remains fall. Drop your opinion like it was a doomsday asteroid, brace for the assault to follow, and enjoy.

Don't worry about offending anyone there, as those most likely to get in your face about it won't worry even the slightest about offending you right back.

Hit them with everything you've got. Let them have it with both barrels, don't say that you can see their point if you really can't. That only gives them a false sense of superiority, like maybe they could turn you to their way of thinking if only they could get your wrong-minded views out of the way, you potential worker bee you. "Never give in except to convictions of honour and good sense. Never yield to force; never yield to the apparently overwhelming might of the enemy," to quote Churchill.

So there, brothers and sisters of the offensive West, is my rant for the week. Take from it what you will, but do not expect me to apologize if it offends you.   It is not my responsibility to thin my skin because you refuse to thicken yours. You are all, at least in theory, worthwhile adults, not spoiled children. Act like it.

A Few Random Thoughts on Those Damnfools Who Want A Revolution

(*The Libertarian Enterprise,* October 21, 2018)

Folks are just going crazy nowadays. Flinging hate and calling it inspired, while doing their best to cut the floor from under the feet of those that they deem "offensive," showing exactly as much courtesy and civility to those that they accuse of having a lack of courtesy and civility. The only consistency is the lack of consistency, in regards to how they want to be treated, weighed against how they treat.

I hate looking at those blathering propaganda machines that pass for news services these days. I'm sure that it's always been the same, but the older I get, the more insane it all sounds. Those that promote whatever political/social slant that best suits their psychosis don't even try to pretend to be unbiased anymore, but rather jump into the crazy pool feet first, with not bricks but fellow citizens bound to their ankles, hoping to drown us with them. I remember the shining days of my teenaged years, when (after a reading of Smith's *The Probability Broach,* and Koman's *The Jehovah Contract*) I cussed at the obvious bigotry of the Clinton News Network, and the right-hating mentality of the major networks, as a golden time of truth and virtue by comparison.

Though what has begun to irk me the most is all of the calls for open revolution coming from (among other, more worthwhile people) the Hollyweird Left. Obviously a cluster of mouth breathers with no sense of history if they think that it would be fun to start a war on their own soil, disregarding the blood already spilled there in two previous civil wars (which the American Revolution *was* until it was won!). The kind of lunatics who look at the Russian Revolution as a good thing, where, for at least a few wonderful, blood-soaked years, the good guys won, only to be shuffled off the world stage for a while by evil capitalists (Never mind the fact that capitalism is the sociopolitical advantage that allows these morons to be rich in the first place).

I look at the news this morning and what do I see? More Amy Schumer (seeking for relevance by getting arrested [sorry: still don't care]). Alec Baldwin calling for the overthrow of the American government like the good little Leninite that he's proven himself to be (but, wait: didn't he promise to leave the country if second Bush won reelection? What are you still even doing here Alec? Still having trouble finding help with the move? I can think of a few thousand folks who'd carry all of your stuff over whichever border you want to cross by hand, if only to get your Pinko posterior off of our sacred soil). Protesters and rioters, knocking down statues, accosting private citizens in restaurants, initiating force upon the persons of those they deem politically or socially unacceptable.

Revolution and overthrow. Blood and carnage, on a scale unseen in the last 150-odd years in this country, where every casualty is an American casualty. Where brother will kill brother, and child their parents. This is what is being promoted by these animals. And make no mistake about it: they are animals. They want your blood because you believe differently than they do. They want your blood if you feel the same, only then your blood will be spilt for a greater cause: them. When someone says that they want to overthrow the government, in their heart of hearts, they will always see themselves sitting in the big seat once it's been vacated. They will chop and rend, and bath in the blood of the vanquished, and smile and dance and sing while they do it. Because that's what they always do. A quick look at revolutionary France, or Russia, or damn near anywhere else where a civil war has been fought will show this. Animals behaving like animals. Violence for its own sake.

Citizens (not subjects) of America, I say to you: Don't fall for it. Prove that you are worthy of the mantle passed down to you by those forbearers that gave their lives, fortunes, and sacred honor so that you could be *Citizens of the Uniter States of America!* Don't be the sheep that the violent left wants you to be. Because, make no mistake, as has always been the case, once their enemies are gone, they will assuredly turn their guns on you.

2022 Update: Alec Baldwin still hasn't left, or stopped taking shots at folks.

<u>The Couch Potato War Correspondent</u>
(*The Libertarian Enterprise,* November 11, 2018)

1. The Fifth of November

I thought I'd try something different this week, and as opposed to writing a short rant in a single sitting, stretch it out over a few days, to inform on myself, and the circles that I stumble through.   I thought I'd do this because, like EVERY election (at least according to the talking [empty] heads of the American news services) the one coming up on Tuesday, November 6, 2018, will be the most important one in our lives.

Let's start there.   I don't believe it.   It will be as important as any other election, no more or less. What this one does have going for it, however, is that wonderful feeling that each vote against the socialist (Democrat) state is just another nail in their coffin. Which is kind of a shame.   I have some pretty good acquaintances (even one friend) who self identify as Democrats, none of whom feels properly represented by the wide-eyed lunatics that pass as the living, breathing, oozing faces of their party.   So then, how have we come to this?   To these violent clowns in expensive suits, calling the restrained Right violent, when it is they, themselves, who are actively, intentionally inciting violence, if not participating in it? I look at it, and can only come to a few conclusions.

For the eight years preceding the last two, the far left had been at the top of the ant hill, with their leader—that would be the unquestionable-unless-you're-racist Saint Barry, in case you were wondering —doing everything in their power to strip those God-given rights not guaranteed but *acknowledged as already being ours in the first place* from us, with smiles on their demonic-cherubic faces, all the while going out of their way to stoke racial hatreds, disrespect of those brave few in our armed forces, chipping away at the process of law, and telling us all the while that it was for our own good, because they love us. So given their feelings of plenty for the better part of a decade, Comrade, is it any wonder that they feel threatened when they don't just see, but feel, the rug being pulled out from under them? It's basic psychology: bullies just hate seeing someone bigger, stronger, better armed, and unwilling to take their crap stroll into the playground.

In short: they hate us. With all the fiber of their being, with every beating of their black, evil hearts, they hate us, and the more than two century old American ideal that we stand for. They hate us for looking at cut-rate, over paid athletes who would kneel during the anthem as the vermin that they are. They hate us for not looking at each violent encounter with a cop on the news and not instinctively knowing that it's gotta be the cop's fault, because, well, y'know: racism, I guess. They hate us. Pure and simple.

We each know about hate, even if it's in a less solid way than the hate that these gomers feel. I do hereby confess, though without the slightest apology, to being a heterosexual, caucasian, right-wing Christian male. It's what I am. As such, depending on what point in my life you would have asked me, I have ideas as to what, or who, I would call The Enemy. If you'd have asked me as a teenager, when I was just another pissy, gun-nut atheist, I'd have told you that the Enemy was the political Left, at that point figure-headed by "Waco Willy" (to borrow a poignant nickname)Bill Clinton, who (as is their habit) wanted nothing more than to rip the foundations from my way of life. As an equally pissy, but somewhat less hormonal, 20-something, I'd have said much the same, but added in my first boss, various family members, and women who'd broken my wittle heart. Looking down 40's tailpipe as I am now, the list has changed a bit to the political Left and their leader Satan.

These are the wankers that I just can't shake. The ones that are shouting at me every time I turn on the tube, check the news services, or check out my mail. I don't see any political pamphlets for the right in my mailbox. I wonder why that is? Maybe because they've already gotten the rational members of society, and feel no need to scrape the sewers to change the minds of the vermin living there? But, I digress.

Two years ago, I stood in a fairly long line outside of our local voting place (a school, not that this stopped the angry Democrats in attendance from yelling swears and threatening violence to the Republicans there) wearing, as I do every election, my *Vote Cthulhu: Why Choose the Lesser Evil* T-shirt, just doing my civic duty. I voted, generally Republican, but wrote in None of the Above for the presidential slot. After the preceding elections, where I'd felt like a whore no matter who I'd voted for (only difference being that I could at least take a cleansing shower after voting Republican), I'd decided not to vote for either of the candidates. The looks that I'd gotten from those in attendance around that school, who'd asked *me* how I was voting, were priceless. I'd have gotten more friendly faces if I'd answered Hitler than what I told them. I expect more of the same tomorrow.

Because, you see, for the first time since I started voting at the age of 18, I will be voting straight Republican. Make no mistake: I still am not a fan of the Donald. As a person. He still strikes me as a slimy, New York creep. But I have surprisingly little issue with his politics. He surprised me two years ago by winning, and has continued to surprise me to this day by doing (gasp!) exactly what he said he'd do if elected. He's kicking over anthills, shaking the trees of political lifers, and seems to be going out of his way to reaffirm the Bill of Rights as the highest law in the land, and not merely a bunch of kinda-sorta suggestions written down by some racist honkies two hundred-odd years ago.

Tomorrow I vote, for better or worse. I do not think that this will kill the Democratic party. Though I suspect that it will mobilize those mental deficients that make up the majority of its membership (especially those in high office), and as such, I will be armed and ready to repel borders, should they have the bad idea to attempt a straightforward coup, as opposed to the slow chipping away that they've been attempting for two years now. How will it all go? Suppose I'll have to wait till tomorrow to see.

2. November 6: Judgment Day

The Shirt on, I packed my kids up this morning and drove the whole three minutes over to the elementary school that serves as our voting place. It was raining, like the sky itself was mourning the passing of one side or another. Or maybe it was shedding tears over the death of civility in the land. Or maybe I'm just feeling melancholy and poetic. Thank God I don't drink anymore, or this could take a maudlin turn.

My youngest daughter asked me where we were going, and when I told her she got very excited. I wasn't sure exactly why until her face got that sad-dissapointed-let-down expression, and let me know she thought I'd said "Boating," not "Voting." I haven't got the heart to tell her that disappointment is what most folks feel when discussing politics. Life will teach her that lesson all on its own, and her inner cynic will come charging to the front, making her old man look like an optimistic birdbrain.

When I voted two years back, there was a nice crowd gathered outside. Nice in size if not in manner. This year only a single Republican and Democrat braved the elements outside. Surprising, since I always assumed that water melted the Left, which is why I was always confused by their reluctance to colonize nearby planets and moons, with their comparable lack of water. Though, in complete honesty, both were fine, gentlemanly folks, neither of whom I took issue with at these brief meetings.

Inside the school, I was met by staff, each older men and women well into the second half of their century of life. Always professional, they were nevertheless cordial and helpful, making a big deal out of my children being with me, and how important it was to install the love of voting at an early age, lest we breed more voter apathy. To which I replied, "Yep." Once in the booth, the actual voting was done with quickly—to which my oldest asked, "Is that it?"—and the three of us were given our *I Voted* stickers, to wear all day, volunteering how we voted to anyone who bothered to ask.

Over the past few hours I've looked at the news (turning into a sadist in my old age), only to see exactly what I've expected. Democratic victories surge, apparently, despite the fact that voting isn't finished, or the churning idea that has taken root in my mind that the exit pollers only bother to ask the folks who look most Democratic how they voted.

Amazing, y'know, how 200 % of the vote is for the Left so far, screw you very much border wall promoting, racist, sexist, Right wing wankers, you.

In truth, I doubt very much that I'll wait up long enough to hear the results. I may be woken in the middle of the night by gunfire as the losing Left, peaceful as they are, take their loss with as much grace and decorum as I expect from them, firing off the first shots in the Civil War that they are begging for. Though I'm not too worried about that where I'm at. Even the neighbors that I've got who aren't Republicans aren't Democrats. At least I don't think so. They do have jobs, after all.

So, then: onward toward tomorrow, when we find out the fate of the world, or some such. God be with us.

3. November 7: The Pieces, and Where They Fall

So things didn't turn out quite like so many of us would have hoped, but it could have been much worse too. What is completely hilarious to me—in a squirmy-skin, get these vile creeps out of my face before I stomp on them kind of way—is the inevitable way in which the Left media are reacting to last night's vote.

Without singling out any single "news" service (they know who they are, in much the same way that sexual predators do; and care about as much), I was whelmed to see headlines touting the bravery of those newly elected Democrats, who will no longer have to be afraid of The Donald or his racist ways! Afraid? Did I miss something?

It seems to me that over the past two years, I have seen little fear—unless whining and screaming and begging for armed insurgencies counts as fear—from most of the Left. Or the Right for that matter.

What I have seen is a bunch of mealy mouthed psychopaths calling for civil war, before the first active words as President were out of Trump's mouth.   I saw endless cries of "He's not my president!" (Sorry, though: because he *is*, regardless of how you feel about him, unless you (please God) renounce your citizenship and move to any of the places around the globe that you believe to be better than here. And if they're so much better, don't you owe it to your children, not to mention yourself to go there? Wouldn't doing anything less be child abuse, if you could get them out of what you see as an intolerable, hostile situation? Or are you just running at your mouths, without a shred of integrity behind your words, you inconsistent bastards?)   I have heard Party leaders telling their brainwashed followers to corner and attack those on the other side of the isle, all the while claiming that it is those same Right-leaning officials that are the ones promoting violence. Inconsistency? Hell, no: Democratic at its perpetually more Left-leaning best!

In truth, I see very little change coming in the future. The Democrats in Washington will do their best to gum up the works, as they've gone out of their way to do over the past two years, while the Republicans will go about their business like usual, wearing helmets to protect themselves from those who see the blather of Clinton and Schumer and Waters as the handed down from on high words of Marx… er, I mean God.

So, to all of you out there in internet land, those few who are still in a proper state of mind—one might even say a *Right* state of mind—all I have to say in closing is this: keep your heads up, your brains on, and your powder dry. As I've said before, you're citizens, not subjects. Embrace it, make it who you are, and be ready to keep the world a place where you will be proud to have your children, grandchildren, and more live and grow and embrace their own freedoms.

-Amen.

*2022 Update: Wow, if I'd have known then how much worse things would have gotten in only four years, I'd have bought a helmet of my own. In the last year, after an unquestionably stolen election, the professional American left (and their owners, the world's Communist states) have gone out of their way to punish the citizens of this great land. How dare we think and breath and act for ourselves! I am firmly of the opinion, after the last fourteen months of fascist dictates being handed down by Pedo Joe, on behalf of whoever owns him, that there's nothing trustworthy about liberals, at all, ever. Those that still speak up on behalf of this monster, or any of his only technically human ilk, are beyond saving. May God have mercy on their souls.

(*The Libertarian Enterprise,* November 11, 2018))

Open question: does anyone—*should* anyone—care what celebrities have to say about anything at all? I suppose you could care if they were thespians, good at their work, true professionals, who you've asked for advice in regards to acting. Likewise painters, pool players, and other similar worthies. Don't get me started on if athletes are worth listening to in any respect, given their already enlarged senses of worthiness and entitlement, all the while promoting gang mentality and violence for its own sake. But this misses the earlier question: should we care what thoy all think otherwise?

Politicians, whose opinions on politics are hardly worth mentioning as so many—the pessimist in me says *most*—care about nothing more than becoming a lifer, are paid with our tax dollars to talk about politics and (apparently) rip our Constitutional rights from us. Politics is their job, and I hardly care what they have to say about the color of grass. That being the case, how much more do I care about what Clooney, Sarandon, or any of that bitter lot feel, or think, at all? Heck, I'm not really concerned with what folks like Ted Nugent and Kurt Russell think, and I like them.

So, given that I—and no one is an audience of one so I have to assume that I'm far from alone in this—wish that they would just shut the hell up, why is it so hard for the Hollywood Left to keep their gobs closed? Are the Right wing celebrities as mouthy, and the news services just don't report it because they're too busy waiting for Saint Barry to walk on water? I find that hard to believe. Heck, every other thing a Right winger says is on the news right away, twisted into some kind of sexist, racist hate monologue, so why not their rationalized politics? I think I've got a theory.

See, when the Right come to a conclusion, they come to it through thought, process of elimination, and deep soul-searching. Their opinions aren't grounded on wet newspaper, but on foundations of stone and brick. That being the case, given the hole-brained thugs that pass as investigative reporters nowadays, when they are confronted with the hows and whys of their beliefs, they can back them up.

It feels different with the Left. Listening to them, it is all a hodgepodge of anti-Trump, pro-free health care, pro-Big Brother, ant-Constitution nonsense that they might as well have read on the back of a box of cereal packaged by LBJ or Uncle Joe Stalin. They repeat by rote, with never an original thought in their heads, but with a fanaticism that would have made the Nazi youth proud.

And Lord are they getting desperate. And dumb. With no idea of how money works. They seem to have missed that bit about nothing being free. Everything is paid for somewhere. Free healthcare? Why not, we'll just tax the middle and upper classes until we're all destitute. But hallelujah, at least we'll all have the same cut-rate, crap, government insurance! Victory!

Again: back to the question: why do we listen? Is it because we have nothing better to do? Waiting for the pizza to be delivered, we just need to watch the idiot box, putting up with whatever nonsense is on, rather than picking up a book? Better to be entertained than enlightened? Crap. I can't believe that we've gone that far down the rabbit hole. We're Americans, damn it! We fought the tide of Communist oppression for fifty years, and by God we won! Are we only going to let all of that go, now, electing them into office, without their having to even hide what they are?   How in the name of God did Sanders or Ocasio-Cortez even get on the ballet? Our predecessors are rolling over in their graves today.

So how did we get here? Where did we go wrong? I suppose that so much of it comes down to that ol' fallback, the Cult of Personality. Heinlein (at least I assume it was him; Lord knows I see his name attached to the meme enough) said "[T]here seems to have been an actual decline in rational thinking. The United States had become a place where entertainers and professional athletes were mistaken for people of importance. They were idolized and treated as leaders; their opinions were sought on everything and they took themselves just as seriously-after all, if an athlete is paid a million or more a year, he knows he is important ... so his opinions of foreign affairs and domestic policies must be important, too, even though he proves himself to be ignorant and subliterate every time he opens his mouth." So here we have a cluster of self-important less-worthy-than-thous who are so sure of their inherent greatness that they need to save us from ourselves, like the fascists always do. And they are met with open arms and empty minds by that always present portion of the population that would rather follow the devil into hell than make up their own minds about anything at all.

Sickening tough this may be, it is hardly anything new.   There have always been leaders, followers, and leave-me-aloners, for all of human history. Why should now be any different. What we have to do is what great individualists have always done: rise above.   Inform ourselves.   Recognize threats for what they are and act accordingly. Become the ideal human subject, the one who sees the world with open eyes, and bends knee to no one other than God and the woman we're proposing to.

And don't forget to put your money where your mouth is. If there is someone that you find to be politically or personally repugnant, don't fork over the cash to embrace their product.   Save it for some other, more worthy, purveyor of entertainments and insights.   There are many.   Walk past the endless barrage of Stephen King doorstops, and buy Heinlein, Koontz, Smith, or someone else whose work doesn't make you feel greasy after you're done with it. Ditch out on the Clooney flick, they're always pretentious and lackluster anyway, and pick *Alongside Night*, *The Thing from Another World*, or *The Wrath of Khan*. You'll feel better if you do.

The New-Old Happyday Bloodbath
(November ,2018)

Recently a science fiction/fantasy writer that I enjoy posted on his Fakebook feed that it's time for the Constitution to be looked at in a more progressive way. Well, now…

I suppose that I should fess up to being more than a bit hypocritical in regards to judging writers for their shortcomings.   I'm much harsher with actors, and judge most professional athletes before they even open their mouths (an admitted prejudice on my part). Yet, when it comes to writers, especially good ones, I tend to turn a blind eye more often than not. I suppose that it's because I have nothing but respect for someone who can delve into the mind of a diverse cast of characters, and show me how they think, and why they do the things they do.   As such, I can forgive a lot.

Sometimes it works out. If not for that blind eye, I never would have discovered Mack Reynolds, one of the shining giants (for me at least) of the silver age of science fiction.   Or Harlan Ellison, for that matter. But what Reynolds and Ellison, and a lot of their left-wing contemporaries, had going for them, that most of those who work in the field today don't, is that they could spin a story that held you in your seat like you were buckled there. The story was first, and if some deeper moral was there, more's the better.

So, yes: sometimes it works out. Some times it doesn't.

My hypocrisy has, over the past two years, put me in a position to have to listen (or read) words of irrational hate coming from those minds that I had so admired. To see the degradation of intellects that

I had come to look for inspiration in. There is nothing but hate there now, and it reflects in their work to such an extent that story has not just taken the back seat, it has been left by the roadside to make more room for the exact kinds of "Hate Speech" that they rally against.

My reading list of living writers has been significantly decreased recently.

If you'd have asked me three or four years ago what living writers I read, the list would have been short.   Smith, Koman, Schulman, Koontz, Robert Crais, Michael Connelly, Harlan, Pournelle, Niven, and those few whose works I have recently washed my hands of. In the intervening years, we've (and when I say "we've" I mean we as in the human race) lost some giants, who wrote some of the most inspiring, teeth-kicking, nerve-rending pieces of literature the world has ever seen. So when those couple of writers that I still bother with write something new, I don't just look forward to it with entertainment as the forethought. I look to them, as well, with hope, of not just good words, characters, plots, but also of a craft the headliners of which seem in a sorry state to progress.

But all of this gets me off of my initial point, which is: No, we do not need to look at the Constitution of the United States of America in a more progressive way. Because, you see, to look at it in what is today considered to be a progressive way is to strip the intent from it.   It is to look back on decades of Cold War and say, "Just kidding. You can win."   I'm sure that those who fought with the Red hordes in Russia early in the last century thought they were being incredibly progressive, right up until their fascist saviors turned the bayonet on them. I'm certain that those removed from service by Stalin in the purges figured themselves wonderfully progressive.   Likewise the followers of Hitler. Likewise the impressionable fools who look to Sanders and Clinton and their ilk to save them.

Here's the rub, though: the only thing that lubricates the wheels of their kind of progress in the blood of the masses. In case you missed it: that's us. You and me and every other Joe or Jane who works for a living. Hype to the contrary they will not bleed for you. That's not their intention. The machine only grinds one way, until you turn it off. It's past time to do so.

So, Left-wing writers of the USA, please reclaim your sanity, your souls! Learn to write again, before you throw it all away. Your saviors are false prophets, using you as the mouthpieces of their hateful, insurrectionist propaganda.   Don't trick yourselves, don't allow yourselves, to be tricked into thinking otherwise.

*2022 Update: with the passing of so many of the greats over the last few years, and the retirement of others due to medical misfortunes, a good book by a good writer is more golden now than ever before. Though make no mistake: There's still good stuff out there. I can still look forward to Chuck Dixon, Mike Baron, F. Paul Wilson, Robert Crais, Michael Connelly, and other worthies. Thank the Lord.

Welcome to the Shit Show

(The Libertarian Enterprise, December 1, 2018)

Being offended has been effectively weaponized by the political Left. This should come as no surprise to anyone who has payed attention over the last fifty years, with Orwell and Dick using the idea to such effect, but the incredible way that this weapon of opportunity has been used by those opponents of freedom that are pasted across every news source is truly staggering.

Things have gotten so far out of hand that no one seems able to say anything without offending someone, whether there was offense meant or not, that multiplo times daily there are headlines shrieking, "This-or-that talentless actor/sports 'star'/ politician apologizes to weak-kneed noodle for uttering anything close to an opinion." And maybe I'm seeing what I want to see, but it seems to me that those offering these enabling "So sorry"'s are disproportionately Right-wing.

Why is that? Is it that the Left are simply so much more sensitive that the rest of us? Or are they using this automatic offense so liberally to keep anyone from actually saying anything at all? Perhaps it's just me, but I am offended countless times every time a Democrat, or Socialist, or Democratic Socialist (damnfools that they are) opens their spewing gobs, but have never demanded an apology from any of them. Point of fact, the only people that I insist on hearing apologies from are my own children, in an attempt to make them think more about the words they say in the future.

Churchill once said, "You have enemies? Good. That means you've stood up for something, sometime in your life." This mentality seems to be lost on modern times. We as a species are so terrified of saying the wrong thing that we're terrified of saying anything. There was an old line about never discussing religion, politics, or red-headed women in polite company as you never know who you're going to offend. They used to call it manners. And don't get me wrong, there's something to being polite, to not going out of your way to make those in your company uncomfortable. But there's a difference between this kind of belief, and zipping your lip when some slack-jawed buffoon is going out of their way to crap on everything you hold deer.

Yet we still shut our mouths, for fear of offending, for fear of the repercussions that might follow our social faux pas of saying something with real worth behind it. And it's not just in politics that we've been neutered. Recently I was informed that my stating my opinions as facts was making some of those around me uncomfortable. Really? Saying what I believe like I actually believed it? What a novel idea. Seems to me that putting a little *God willing* behind what we say is a good thing every now and then. But I'm a hypocrite, aren't I? Instead of pushing back, instead of going out of my way to make my points verbally to those that I have apparently offended, I retreated into these words, blathering on in a way that those on the other side of my argument will never see. Woe to the world if I ever grow a backbone…

But I digress.

So, with the defeat of Abrams in Georgia, Hollyweird has once again shown their true colors, calling for a boycott of the state, thereby taking from it revenues because the west coast Left didn't get their way. Because they're offended by democracy in action. Because democracy isn't socialism. Sounds fair, right? Because if roles were reversed it'd still go down the same way, wouldn't it? If Abrams had won, and those few Right-minded actors, directors, producers, etc., had boycotted Georgia, there wouldn't be any kind of ramifications, would there? There would be no calls of bigotry, racism, sexism, or any of the other -ism's that the Left pull out EVERY SINGLE TIME they don't get their way. Because the American Left is nothing if not fair-minded.

Our way or the shit-show. That's the prevailing mentality of the American Left. Do what we say, give us our way, or else. And that "or else" is the taking away of our lives, liberties, and pursuits of happiness.

We, as freedom-loving citizens of the United States of America have two choices, as I see it. We can buckle under, give them their way, and say goodbye to the Great Experiment that this country represents. Or, we can brace our feet, take the brunt, say, "No," and regain our God-given rights. We can be upstanding human beings who are not afraid to offend, to say what we mean, and stand by it.

Don't be afraid to offend, to make enemies with your thoughts and opinions. All that means is that you've said stood for something, some time in your life. Besides, you might actually do those on the Left some good , forcing their skin to thicken up, to join the rest of us in a future worth living in.

<u>**Why It Matters**</u>

(*The Libertarian Enterprise,* December 9, 2018)

L. Neil Smith brought me here. I'm undoubtedly not the first person to have said those words, nor will I be the last. Because this magazine has been instrumental in saving the minds of countless people over the years. It has been responsible for letting those of us who fit neither into the square-peg Right, nor the Hammer and Sickle Left, that we are not alone. There are many of us out there, lovers of freedom as more than an abstract concept, who have looked to this modest enough tome and smiled knowingly.

Through the Libertarian Enterprise, I was introduced to the works of J. Neil Schulman, the late Victor Milan, and Sarah Hoyt, and through them to other greats like Victor Koman, Stephen Hunter, and John Ross. Writers who not only entertained me, but managed to enlighten me, inform me, anger me, and make me question things. They explained in ways that a snotty 17-year old could understand the core of Libertarian philosophy and political thought.

Back in 1997 when I was first introduced to TLE it was like a breath of fresh air. I'd already given up on reading newspapers, and could find very little online that satisfied my need to learn. Enter my uncle who over a few months passed on not only copies of *The Probability Broach* and *The Jehovah Contract*—years after truly screwing me up by giving me his copies of various Heinlein classics, along with Keith Laumer, Dean Koontz, and many others—but who pushed issue after issue of TLE at me, knowing that it would grab, and boy was he right.

There comes a point in anyone's life, I think, when they first discover politics when they become unbearable to all of those around them. It is during this time that you know who your real friends are (hint: they're the ones who still talk to you once you pass through the fires of political fanaticism). It's when you begin to mold who you are going to be as an adult: A bottom-feeder Liberal, who feels that they have every right to get hold of their "fair" share of what you sweat and bleed to earn; a hard-hearted, though not as tough as you make out to be Conservative; or something other, better.

Thank God that I leaned toward this last. Thank God I decided that I don't have any right to what morally belongs to someone else. Thank God that I never let the thin steel get into my blood, making me heartless, and unaccepting. I learned to judge people by their choices, to bother with or not bother with folks based on their merits as people, disregarding everything else.

The Libertarian Enterprise started me down this road.

Which is not to say that the road has always been easy. In the early 2000's, I became so infuriated with the Libertarian Party figureheads, and their, to me, bassackwards politics that I turned off. When the political party that formed my hopes for the future looked to be turning away from a firm conviction that the Bill of Rights was paramount, toward a more *Don't-mess-with-my-drugs-or-porn-and-you-can-take-away-the-rest-of-my-God-given-rights,-no-problem* kind of mentality, I could have spit.

I went years with my back turned to what I saw as a betrayal, a bastardization of what I had embraced. I lamented the time wasted. In truth, I'd done what I always do. See, as a youngster, I'd done the same thing with religious belief.   I'd hated organized religion and its "our way or the highway" presentation, and mutated that into a hate for God. It was't until I had it pointed out to me that hating religion and hating God weren't the same thing that perspective came. Likewise, over the past few years, that kind of perspective came to my view of politics.

To look at the meaningless figureheads of all political parties, and blame the followers of the body politic can be so foolish.   Reading this incredible cyber magazine weekly can prove that. Each week I am brought ideas that embrace those beliefs that first brought me to politics in the first place. I get to read the thoughts of people, smarter than me, whose words have moved, and continue to move, me. These things are important.

What we have here is pure love.   Love of freedom. Love of integrity. Love of learning. We are visited every seven days by folks that have more in common with us, over thousands of miles, than we have with many who are blood relations. This is as much a family gathering, as the worlds best, most intelligent, fan convention. It brings more and more people to the cause of freedom every time a new issue is published.

Over the past couple of months, it has been my absolute honor to see my words published alongside those that so helped to mold me into the man that I am today. If I never write another word, I can be contented to know that some of those that I've already scribbled are here, to be enjoyed by posterity.

I sometimes delude myself into thinking that somewhere along the line, some otherwise intelligent 17-year old might read something that I've written, and be turned on to the Libertarian philosophy. In all likelihood, it'll never happen.   My words aren't impressive, or moving, enough.   Doesn't matter, though, does it? If it never happens again, it at least happened the once.

To me.

So, L. Neil, TLE, and all others involved in actively making the world a better, more liberty-minded place, on the momentous event of your 1,000th issue: thank you.

<u>**Heroics and Hypocrisy**</u>
(*The Libertarian Enterprise,* December ,2018)

In one of his voluminous introductions (always a high point of any of his collections of incredible yarns and essays) Harlan Ellison introduced me to the concept of Heroification. This concept, as I understand it, is the act of looking up to a person so much as to see in them nothing short of a demigod, a luminary creature more shining example of perfect humanity than actual human. In his case, he was referring to Gene Roddenberry. He may as well have been talking about how modern Communists look at their still recently deposed godhead, Saint Barry.

Every time the various news services post a new piece about the former Commander In Chief, they may as well insist that their readers or viewers shield their eyes so as to not gaze directly upon the holy visage. While the man (term loosely used) is actively undermining the role of the Presidency, they cheer him on, chanting his name, waiting for that long-prophesied (two years is a long time to those who would destroy history) day when he will walk across the water to take his rightful place upon the Throne of Earth (where he belongs anyway, right?).

We shouldn't be at all surprised by this deviant behavior, though. I mean, we're talking about the beastly person who went out of his way to stoke racial strife, undermine public faith is police, and systematically rape the Bill of Rights for eight long years, accompanied by the cheering, condoning chorus of the world media. It didn't matter what he did wrong, he did nothing wrong. He could have burned the flag, and sprayed waste across the ashes, and those subhumans that present the "news" to us every day would have not only shouted their approval, but would have brought the marshmallows to roast over the accompanying fires lit by the fascist and kindled with the Constitution, the Declaration of Independence, and anything else that may come to hand, just so long as it was something of worth, something that had helped us become Americans, By God!

Which is not to say that Saint Barry is the first one that they've canonized. I remember them doing the same thing to Bill Clinton back in the nineties. I was twelve when Saint Willy took office, and through him I experienced my first instances of Presidential hate. I hated Bill Clinton. No other word for it. I hated him as much as the excusing media loved him. I saw nothing good in his every action, and lies in his every word. I felt toward Clinton the same way that the modern media filth mongers hate The Donald, and with as much fanaticism.

Difference? I was a child, and I got over it. I still don't like Saint Willy, but I far from hate him. All it takes is a look at history (see how that keeps coming up to understand the world? Are you listening CNN and your propagandizing ilk?) to see how many ill-suited folks have held high office. Contemporary talking heads will tell us that Washington, Jefferson, Reagan, anyone right-leaning, were nothing but racists, homophobes, and baby-killers. Though they continue to put others, less worthy, up on pedestals. Woodrow Wilson? Drove us into a war after promising us that he wouldn't do so as part of his platform? FDR? Don't get me started. He couldn't have done more to keep the Depression going if he'd gone out and taken folk's money himself. LBJ? Just another SOB, and far from the savior riding in on a white horse that movies and documentaries seem dead set on presenting him as.

I guess it's the same for everybody, though. That first president that you remember actively disliking is the one that becomes the burning example of everything that's wrong with those who lust for power. But, jeez, aren't I lucky to live in a time when the Democratic Party is going out of their way to give us candidates of such raw, low caliber. Rapists, racists, and hate-mongers. Exactly what they call their opponents.

The media while covering the funeral of George H. W. Bush took many an opportunity to turn a time of mourning into a hack job, wherein they attempted to discredit The Donald for the (shocking!) act of ignoring his former opponent, Hillary Clinton. After their constant, endless, cries of his supposed interactions with Russians and criminals, you'd think that they would be happy to see him ignoring one for a change, but there's just no making some folks happy.

But understand why I bring up the funeral in the first place. Their hatred of Trump is every bit as morbid as their love of Saints Willy and Barry. During his four years in office, those same talking heads that were praising the goodness and kindness and presidential stature of George H. W. Bush after his passing were the same ones who demonized him when he was the Commander in Chief! He wasn't Jimmy Carter, or LBJ, or (after the fact) Clinton, so he was obviously a blip in history, not worth really noticing, unless it was to cast criticism at him.

It could be a case of The Grass Is Always Greener, but I don't think so. I feel, truly and in my heart, that the idea behind these constant attacks on Republican presidents is nothing less than an attempt by the Left Wing powers that be to destroy the party, thereby paving a smooth way for a perpetual Democratic presence in the Oval Office. They would *gladly* stand back and grin while a permanent Democratic (here see: Communist, as they are hiding their true selves less and less as the days go on, up to and including the election of self-proclaimed Democratic Socialists) dictatorship in Washington.

They mourned the passing of the Soviet Union, so is it any wonder that they would want to reinstall the fragile foundations of that failed experiment in Evil here?

A relative of mine, a smarter person than I'm ever likely to be, postulated a theory to me that I cannot completely shake off. He said in passing to me the other day that he believed that Saint Barry and Holy Mother Michelle had opted to remain in DC so as to make it easier to move back into the White House once the Democratic coup took place. Paranoid, right? Or is it?

Try as I might, I just can't shake the feeling that should such a coup take place, there'd be countless millions waiting in the streets to throw down palm fronds in front of them, while others took the time to destroy the Washington and Jefferson Memorials, and burn the Smithsonian to the ground. They'd throw out the Spirit of '76, in favor of the Memory of 1917. Not because it's some new kind of idea, but because it's always what they've done. For decades they rolled over for the Soviets. In more recent times, they stood behind them. At this point, they stand beside them. And the figurehead of this psychotic embrace of a constantly failed, dangerous, murderous political ideology is that devious snake, that grinning, hate filled monster, Saint Barry Obama.

<u>**Modern Man**</u>
(*The Libertarian Enterprise,* December 2018)

I read a lot. A few dozen books a year, give or take. When working a third shift job a while back, during which I was guarding a gate in the middle of nowhere where no one ever arrived, I'd sit on the roof of the guard shack under the clicking-clacking overhead lights and read a book and a half a night. I'm fairly well versed in the classics, though I have little time for most of them, with the exceptions of H. Rider Haggard, Jules Verne, Edgar Rice Burroughs, and just about everybody that came out of John W. Campbell's golden age. Though with all of that reading, at this point accumulating into the many millions of pages, I read very little of what is being published right now.

Why is that? There are many folks who are first rate writers being printed now, many (if not most) writing for TLE. But besides them, there's Dean Koontz, Robert Crais, Michael Connelly, Brad Meltzer, and a handful of others. So what makes their writing better than others who burden us with their endless repetitions of the same nihilistic plots? In a word: people.

The characters who people the very best works of fiction, the ones who stick with you years, even decades, after closing the book are the ones that you can understand. Even the most bizarrely fantastical of the lot, the Lazarus Long's and Captain Nemo's and Elijah Baley's, are folks that you can grok because they are, first and foremost, people. They are flawed, yes (unless they're John Carter, who never set a foot wrong, even while setting a foot wrong), but they are not defined by their flaws. They had grit, some steel in their spines and spit in their eyes.

This is missing in many of todays supposedly great characters. I won't name any specifics, as this isn't meant to be a hatchet piece, but suffice it to say that so much of the milquetoast that passes for first rate fictional heroes are anything but. But, given the world of political correctness pushed to the point of absolute insanity where literally everything is offensive, how can they be? The characters have been spayed and neutered and whitewashed in an attempt to not get on anyone's bad side to such an extent that they might as well be shapeless gray forms with barcodes attached. There's nothing there.

Likewise to see a character with anything forming a personal opinion (see: one not decided in committee) is something only villains do. Unless that opinion is that Republicans are stupid, following a President that is evil. That's all good. Be tolerant, though only of the intolerant. Anyone else, anyone who looks at the world as shades of gray, with no defined sense of right or wrong, where no one is to blame for their actions as we are all victims of society (except those victims of victims of society), is off limits. They're enlightened, don't you know.

I haunt used book stored like a ghost. Every so often I turn up a gem. An Asimov that I haven't read yet. A Murray Leinster short story collection. One of Richard C. Meredith's lost, underrated classics. I revel in these. I revel in them because I can understand the people that move through them. I understand the geniuses in Isaac Asimov's books not because I am particularly smart, but because they are worthwhile people. Likewise Leinster; likewise Heinlein, Dick, and the plethora of old guys (and gals) who could (on their worst day) write worlds around what passes for 95% of the best sellers that I am plagued by. I revel in it because it's proof to me that there was a world, once upon a time, when folks were rational, decent, and consistent. When people were polite, yet still willing to stand up and make a point they felt needed to be made, offense be damned. I'm a relatively young guy. I missed out on most of that world. Yet it still exists. There. In dusty old paperbacks with fifteen cent cover prices. And I refuse to believe that it'll never exist again.

*2022 Update: The list gets smaller every day, it seems. With the recent passings of L. Neil Smith and P.J. O'Rourke, most of the giants are gone. But still a few remain, thank God.

<u>**Can-Do**</u>
(*The Libertarian Enterprise,* January, 2019)

I am an American. That single fact alone is enough for me to be hated by many, from those in other countries that see our prosperity and hunger for personal freedom and are disgusted by it, to those fellow citizens who reap the benefits of citizenry all the while lamenting the country that gives them the ability to hate it without jail time, torture, or death.

I love those God-given freedoms guaranteed by the Bill of Rights as much as those opponents of freedom hate them. I exercise my freedom of speech every time someone asks me for my honest opinion, and each time I see something that makes it impossible for me to keep my mouth shut. I respect the freedom of others to do the same, no matter how poorly managed their minds are, or how evil their thoughts, just so long as their idiot ramblings do not hamper my own efforts at personal expression.

Like so many of us, I come from a long line of Americans. We were not all the conservative-leaning folks that we are now. Though I have a cousin that told me once that it was his goal to become an "Arch-Conservative," it was recently revealed to me that I had in my genetic background at least one honest to goodness Huey Long Democrat. And while the thought of sharing the wealth sickens me, I don't feel like my skin is crawling at this notion. Being earlier in the 20th century, during the Depression no less, it is easy to see how someone, even an intelligent someone (as anyone related to me must have been) could have fallen into the mind trap of financial Socialism. We didn't have decades of tried and true Evil to look back on, as we do now.

Which is what makes me so angry about the current bumper crop of so-called Democratic Socialists. They have apparently decided to ignore history, to erase those spots that kill their case for them, in favor of a pipe dream that, if left to its own devices, will be the end of the American dream.

Let's just be clear in this: socialism has never worked. Not once in the last century and a quarter. It has left countless millions starving, hurting, and dead. It has steamrolled the individual, and their rights, until we have a road paved with the bones and blood of the masses. Anyone who does not, or will not, acknowledge this simple, indisputable fact is either an idiot or a liar. So look at those unworthies filling the capitol now and ask yourself: which are they?

In some cases it's easy to tell. There's a meme going around that makes me giggle. In it there is postulation that the DNC's big plan is to let Alexandria Ocasio-Cortez shout out her insane, steadily idiotic ideas in an attempt to make Joe Biden look better. I laugh to stop from crying, because, let's be real, for anyone with a brain it will take a lot to make Joe look better.

So, no doubt, there are some fools, out to make the world a better place, one disregarded individual freedom and stolen bit of personal property at a time. To make us all so dependent of the federal government that we're honestly afraid to vote them out of power. They take from the Wills and give to the Won'ts, and if you call them on it you are a nationalist, racist, bigot, and whatever else they opt to throw at you. And all with the best of intentions, as most of these beasts start. They insist on shutting up the opposing masses to help out those others who follow in their red stride.

Yes, there are fools. But there are also those others.   Those mostly educated beasts who look back on the last 30-odd years and lament the passing of their sacred USSR. The ones who rooted for the Communists under their breaths, who looked down when the flag was held high. These are the folks who cursed Reagan not because they were afraid that he might get us into a nuclear war, but because he was winning! How dare he so expertly undo what Carter spent four hateful years doing?

Make no mistake: they hate America, and everything that it stands for. They hate every word of the Bill of Rights, but none so much as those guaranteeing the right to keep and bear. They want us to be suckling sheep, begging at the government teat. If you keep your distance, or don't hold out your hand to await what they consider your share then you are an enemy of their State.

But these people are nothing new. From the dawn of time there have been monsters. Bloodletters who have sought out the viscera of their fellow beings.   They crop up whenever folks become too complacent.   Whenever a vocal minority becomes too dependent, or wants to be taken care of more than they want to take care of themselves. It always goes the same way: collectivism, statism, sacrifice in the name of the greater good, and the blood that follows. Yet there's hope: because it always ends the same way too. Look to the fall of Soviet Russia. Or, more gloriously, look to the American Revolution.

See, we are Americans, and above all else we achieve. We've brought flight to humanity, and stepped foot on the moon.   There is nothing we cannot achieve. It's in us, down to a cellular level. We do because we can, come hell or high water, and those who would stop that attitude, who would attempt to make us feel guilty for the locational miracle that gave us this country to call home are beasts, monsters. They are the worst that humanity has to offer. And they are *not* Americans.

<u>Can We Chat for a While?</u>

I wrote my first "book" when I was about eight years old: a twelve-page beast of a thing with knights, evil kings, elves, robots, and a large red self-destruct button inspired by some old Iron Maiden album cover and watching the first Terminator at too young an age. I was so proud of the thing. I even begged my oldest sister to take it to school with her to type it up and print it out, so that I could proudly give copies over to everyone I knew, which amounted to family too polite to turn me down. I look back on it now and cringe. It's terrible.

By the time I was seventeen I was submitting short stories to magazines. This synced up perfectly with the worst bout of insomnia that I've ever had to deal with. One, maybe two, hours of sleep a night, for weeks on end with one terrible weekend-long crash. At the end of one of these, with the crash in sight and the room spinning, I decided to sit down in front of my typewriter and kick out a little story. At two or three in the morning, as my folks later informed me. The end result was a short story (less than a thousand words) that I titled "Mr. Peabody and the Headless Boy," which, I will attest until the day I die, is the single best thing I've ever written.

Very proud of this little gem, I submitted it. Much to my chagrin, no one was interested. Fantasy and Science Fiction? Nope. Analog? Nada. Weird Tales? My personal favorite: "Bleak, incoherent, and hard to follow." I still have that rejection letter in a box in my attic.

Long story short: it hasn't seen the light of day, unless you happen to be a good friend, or relative. Until later this year, but more on that later.

Like so many folks, I guess, I've dreamed of writing a novel since first putting pen to paper. There've been plenty of false starts. A crime novel that let me know inside of the first chapter just how little I know about law enforcement. A horror western that I wrote a detailed outline for, along with the first two-fifths of, amounting to about 120 pages, and which I fully intend to finish one day. But the *novel*, as a form of artistic expression, has forever eluded me.

I think it was Koontz who said that agents dislike working with short story writers, as they see them as amateurs, unable to give them the 100,000 words that they are looking for. So, that's me: the perpetual amateur, with delusions of grandeur. However, I will always defend those delusions, as what in the name of God are the good of delusions of mediocrity?

So, two hundred short stories, twelve sales, later, I am looking at the authors proof of my second book. How did I get here?

About ten years back I decided to attempt an intellectual exercise: to outline a long story, with a defined beginning, middle, and end. A science fiction epic for readers of all ages, full of action, adventure, heroes, villains, and concepts on a grand scale. Much to my shock I spent the following decade doing just that: outlining. The result? A long story, told over many smaller volumes and related short stories, that in my head is called *The Last War*.

When my friend Chester Haas—cowriter on the first volume of this long story—and I finished up our little book, we were proud of the finished product. When those beta readers that we dropped it on went through the roof for it, our pride grew by leaps and bounds. When I read it to my two awe inspiring daughters and they told me they liked it, I was through the roof. But, as the old saying goes: pride goeth before the fall.

No agent wanted to touch the thing. "Too short," and "too offensive" were phrases that were thrown our way. I still don't understand this last, but then again it takes a lot to offend me.

In my youth I was prone to depression and anxiety, at least in small bursts. These feelings reared their ugly heads once again when it started to look like our work would amount to nothing, with family and close friends being the only folks to read something that I'd had a hand in writing, yet again.

Enter Sarah A. Hoyt.

A well-established and talented writer in her own right, Mrs. Hoyt did me the honor a few months back of accepting my friend request on Facebook (let this be a lesson to you folks out there: yes, writers are just people, but some are fine examples of humanity, and Mrs. Hoyt is one such). Full disclosure: upon friending her, I'd yet to read one of her many works of fiction, having only been exposed to her articles in places like L. Neil Smith's *The Libertarian Enterprise.* Yet, those articles were so incredible that I found, and still find, myself seeking them out with each and every new issue published. So she's a good writer, but here's what's made me a fan for life: when I sent her a message, she answered.

I asked her, very selfishly I admit, if she had any advice for someone trying to get started, and in no time flat she got back to me offering many sage words of advice, arguably the most important of which were: "Go indie, young writer, go indie."

Such a simple thing, words given by a stranger that meant more than those given by most folks that I've known in the flesh much longer, and they changed the way I was looking at this. Sure, it would be nice to be walking through a brick and mortar book store and see something that I've written up on the shelves, but that's just ego. The fine folks at my local library have taken pity on my need to feed the green-eyes monster and have everything that I've every had published up on their shelves, listed, not by editor, but by my name, so that I can drive down the M-rack whenever I want and bask in those few slim volumes whenever I'm feeling down. So, brick and mortar be damned.

And so, last November my first book, *The Children's War,* was published on Amazon Kindle, with an absolutely incredible cover by Mrs. Katherine Derstein.

When I first held it in my greedy little hands, I could have cried. As has been pointed out to me endlessly: yes, it was self-published. I am no less proud. Couldn't care less. It's out there, for the reading public to enjoy or hate to their heart's content, as I'd always imagined it being.

One down.

Coming up in late-February or mid-March will be the second book, *The Great First Impressions Trip*, again with an incredible cover, this one put together by the great Dr. Victor Koman, out of the kindness of his heart, and another great writer who happens also to be a good fella. Coming soon (another three or four months) will be *The Judas Hymn,* a collection of my published short stories, along with a dozen others (including the previously mentioned "Mr. Peabody and the Headless Boy") featuring a downright off-putting cover by Xander Van Hawley.   After that? Lord, lots more.

You see, I've got a big story to tell, and it is my sincere wish to tell it well.

I guess it's getting past time to wrap this up. I've pimped the books to annoyance. I've thanked those folks that've helped me, when I in no way deserved their help (add to that list Samantha Bryant who, when I asked if I could write a guest blog for her said "Yes.") All that is left is to thank you, whoever took a few minutes out of your busy day to read these ramblings from a poor beggar, asking for your business. I hope that you enjoyed our time together.

<u>**Sad Understanding**</u>
(The Libertarian Enterprise, Feb. 3, 2019)

As much as it pains me to be writing this, I can no longer deny that things are looking toward a Civil War more each day. Understand that I do not welcome this, but neither will I shy from the responsibility that each of us share, as freedom-loving Americans, to uphold the Constitution of the United States, and the inalienable rights guaranteed therein. Only a madman looks forward to spilling the blood of his fellow citizens, and I am no madman. But neither am I a pushover that will stand idly by while the Communists that have been elected by an ever-increasingly, intentionally dumbed-down populace jackboot their way into our Lives, while going out of their way to remove our Liberties and Pursuits of Happiness.

I wrote a few months back that only an idiot wants a Civil War, with the inevitable heartache and bloodshed, and it does look like those idiots are pushing for it every day. In two years' time, I fear, we will be at the turning point of our lives, a time that will live in infamy for those generations to follow. Because, you see, I fully expect The Donald to win the 2020 election. Not by a landslide, but as fairly as he won the 2016 election, with the numbers on his side no matter how much the coast-hopping Liberals cry foul. And as soon as that happens I fully expect all hell to break loose.

I fully expect successions—some of which are already being called for—and many attempts on the life of the president. While I hope that none of them are successful, if one were, I can see in out future, without the slightest suspension of disbelief, a cry not of mourning but rather one of joyous celebration.

Because they hate him, fanatically, unconscionably, like they've hated no one singe Reagan.

Though it must be acknowledged that it's not only his blood that they want. First and foremost, they want—*demand*—our total submission to their ideals and whims, like fascists always do. Though there will inevitably be those who will bend knee to tyranny in an attempt to be safe, to not fight the good fight, I have no doubt that the greater majority of those that they would fit with a collar will hunker down, loaded for bear, and get ready for the fight coming their way.

And when the fight comes, it will be terrible. The brainwashed will take up arms against their brothers and sisters, feeling that they must do right in the eyes of Big Brother, just like go-along-to-get-along's always have. They will do their willing part to obliterate those that they love most, for what they see as the greater good. They will lose little, or no, sleep over this. They never do. They lose more than their freedom that day, they lose their humanity, and that essential something that makes us American. The immortal, perfect words of Franklin come immediately to mind: "Those who would give up essential Liberty, to purchase a little temporary Safety, deserve neither Liberty nor Safety." They will have neither, as if the villains win—and make no mistake, they are villains—what happens will be what has always happened. Midnight arrests, black hood abductions, and the removal of anyone and everyone that is dangerous to the public good, as defined by those who own the public.

I hope that this melancholy meditation will amount to nothing, and that the country will regain its sanity, and move away from the same kinds of Red evil that we fought (and defeated) for the better part of the last century. I pray that all of this will turn out to be just a bump in the road of our brilliant Republic, though I'm no longer holding out much hope.

So for anyone who cares, think good thoughts with me. Do what you can to keep things together until cooler heads prevail.

I've made no secret of my feelings toward the Donald. But whatever else may be said about the man, I feel that he's nowhere near as truly Evil as those who have lined up against him. Monsters like Nancy Pelosi, Chuck Schumer, Bernie Sanders, or that putrid media darling Alexandria Ocasio-Cortez. They want you leashed or put down, make no mistake, do not lie to yourself, or convince yourself otherwise.

*2022 update: This one has been rendered null by the 2020 election, during which the Liberal elite stole the office of the Presidency, plain and simple. Though what scares me more than the Democrats installing their doddering old pedophile, racist of a meat puppet into the office, is that I've met many, many folks who, when asked if they thought that he'd won fair and square, replied that they didn't care. It could be proved to them that the whole thing was a sham, and they'd still be OK with it, because Orange Man bad!

Monsters and Empty Heads
(The Libertarian Enterprise, Feb. 3, 2019)

The foundation that our republic stands on—the Bill of Rights—has been under assault by the Democratic party for at least as long as I can remember. In my own lifetime, there's been the attempts of Waco Willy and Saint Barry, which have left a bad taste in more than one mouth. A cursory look at American history will show that they are just more of the same. Carter, Johnson, Roosevelt, and on the other side of the isle Lincoln and others, have gone out of their way to attempt to remove those God-given rights that make us citizens, and not just more subjects. The political elite are that most vile of things: creatures that want power for its own sake. The bitter things that inhabit the capital presently are no exception. If anything, they may actually be worse.

See, however socialist their aims may have been, those that came before at least had the good sense to not call themselves that. More than the political suicide that would have occurred had Barry or Willy come out and proudly proclaimed that they were doing their best to push America in the direction of the sadly fallen USSR (which failed not because of Communism, remember, but because it wasn't *pure* Communism), would have been the physical upheaval of the blessedly armed masses at seeing their beautiful country under the grip of beasts and Red monsters. There used to be a stigma attached to being a Red American ("Better dead than red," and more accurate words have hardly been spoken). At this point in time it no longer exists. In fact, in many corners it's actually a selling point. I'm looking at *you* New York, who as a majority seemed to think that it was a fine idea to elect into office a blathering idiot who proudly declares herself to be a Democratic Socialist, when to be such is little better than declaring yourself to be a child molester. Likewise *you* Vermont for that insane old Commie Bernie Sanders. After more than a decade of his stinking up the place, I have to ask: what is wrong with you?

These monsters—and I do not use the term loosely; those who would stand on the flag and remove the incredible things that it stands for, the freedoms inherent in it, are monsters, in every Marry Shelly sense of the word—are the new media darlings. Those talking empty heads that so many citizens look to for news are so enamored by these creatures that they dote on their every action, and present it like it was the Second Coming, all the while continuing their vile efforts to demonize the likes of Washington and Jefferson, whose shoes they are not worthy of holding. It has been said until I'm sick of saying it that there is ZERO integrity in contemporary media, whether it be left-leaning or right, yet seems to not have been said enough. Because it is a simple fact that seems to have escaped the notice of the vast majority of people. There are those who still turn on CNN or Fox News to see the events of the day, and expect to see fair, unbiased news coverage. Uninformed or self-deluded, you tell me?

Because I have no doubt that once these socialist critters stop blathering on about stealing from the rich, and how we should have our guns taken away (for the greater good, as always) they will do their best to put their words into action, as the Red monsters always do. And once that happens, there won't be a need for State-sponsored media, with its sanitized views of events. There won't be need because the media has already set themselves the task of being the State-sponsored propaganda machine for the America that they hope is coming. They are preparing themselves for that glorious day when the Bill of Rights, and the things guaranteed therein, are a thing of the past.

Not only will the Democratic Socialists and their revolting puppet heads be overjoyed at the passing of the great experiment, they will be pushed to religious frenzy at the idea of a return to national Communism—like that of lamented Russia, but done right this time. A pure Communism, each person a cog in the great social machine, its moving parts lubricated by the blood of those of us who stood our ground and said, "No!"

<u>Rich Man; Poor Man</u>
(*The Libertarian Enterprise Feb. 10, 2019*)

I don't have a lot of money.   That's not bellyaching, it's just stating the place in the financial scam of things where I find myself.   Not a lot of money, but not poor.   In fact, I'd argue the point that I'm rich in life, with my incredible children, incomparable wife, and my own acceptable-at-my-age health.   I have food in my belly, a roof over my head, and books a-plenty. But money? Nope. Don't think I ever have.

Yet, at no point in time have I looked at those who have more than I do and feel that they owe me something. What's theirs is thoirs and good for them. Even if I don't like them, I don't want what's theirs. I didn't earn it, and I try not to be a parasite.

So why is it, then, that there are so many out there, many of whom are better off than I am, who see someone prospering, and their first thought is to punish them for achieving by taking away what's theirs? It isn't because of some kind of social justice, because theft isn't justice.   It isn't to help out their fellow man, as they would never go so far as to take significant amounts from themselves, as they need it more, what with how busy they are stealing from others to help out the greater good.   It's none of these things. Though I will tell you what it is:

Hate.   They hate achievers more than they hate anything.   They look at By-His-Bootstraps mentalities and grimace and gnash their teeth, and they hate, because they are incapable of that kind of grit, because they are lesser things than the rest of us. They are thieves who hide their thievery behind the false face of equality.   Because, as I've said before, and as I will swear to until the day that I die: forced equality *isn't equality!*

It is only an idiot or a villain who looks at the past failures of socialism, communism, or government-enforced social restructuring and sees not failures but near misses, things that they will do better *this time.* I can look as so many of our Representatives in government and see idiots, with a complete lack of historical knowledge—to say nothing of their lack of articulation, daft buffoons who look at Orwell and see utopia—who think that the Cold War was fought over a particularly chilly winter.

But there are far too many of that other kind, that creature that doesn't have to be dehumanized because they make beasts of themselves. To paraphrase Doc. Johnson, they have gotten rid of the pain of being a man. I am unsure if they want to make the United States into a USSR part 2, or if they are so agonized at the perpetual failures of communism, along with the limitless successes of capitalism, that they are trying to sink the ship.

Would they rather burn it all down? I know that they have no problem with the idea of children and the elderly being murdered in the name of progressive America. As such I have little doubt that they are willing to go up, themselves, if for no other reason than to provide the kindling on which we burn.

They are thieves and cowards, but it is more than that. They are belligerent soldiers, actively fighting a war meant to reduce us, as a people, to nothing more than they wish us to be: slaves.

With every new act passed through Congress, we see a country where more and more people are completely dependent on the Fed, less likely to vote them out of office while there's still the chance. If they get their way, one day soon we will all be so utterly dependent on the government that to get them out of our daily lives will be an unworkable thing, possible only through the bloodshed that such social upheavals generate.

We are—even those of us who are particularly active in our small communities—individuals, not worker ants who go along with the status quo and do what they're told, regardless of the idiocy of it. We each look at the world and our places in it with individual eyes and points of view, and they hate us for it.

We are unpredictable, unruly, and belligerent. Thank God for it. Without these traits, and others that identify us as citizens of America, we'd never have won the Revolutionary War, the Cold War, and the daily battles against tyranny that crop up every day from the powers that be. I believe in my heart that we, as a people, are still ready, willing, and able to fight the good fight, for not only our own sakes, but those of our progeny. We are not all empty-headed, hive-minded lunatics. We are a proud people. Proud of our freedoms, of those who fought and died to guarantee them for us. So if we are going to be worthy of those sacrifices, and the chances for greatness that walk hand in hand with them, we need to step up. We need to be the light in the darkness, not the muted voice of quiet acceptance.

The time to be nice is over. The time to stand up and say, "Enough!" is past due. Sad as it is to say it, the war for the heart of America has started, whether we wanted it or not. They—the Left; the socialist filth that would take from you all those things that are yours—started this fight. It's past time we showed them the err of their ways.

Those Who Can't Defend Themselves
(*The Libertarian Enterprise March 3, 2019*)

There are many things that separate Liberals and Conservatives, but for the sake of this little essay, I'd like to dwell on just one: who they're willing to kill.

You can tell a lot about a person based on who they are willing to let go, for whatever reason. Who they are willing to let die is something that defines their morality, or shows their immorality. That's really what this all comes down to.

You see, generally speaking, Conservatives are willing to let adults die. That's those members of society, 18 to 65 years of age, who are ready, willing, and able to serve in some kind of capacity in either the armed forces, or as police officers. Adults, in other words, who have at least an inkling of what they're getting themselves into, and can make a more or less conscious decision that what they might be dying for is worth dying for.

There used to by lots of words for this kind of mind. Patriotic comes to mind. As does the word integrity. While not all Conservatives have these as parts of their being, many do, so much so that they have become almost synonymous with the political Right.

This leads us to those others. The OTHER human (and I use the term loosely). This is the Liberals. Who are they willing to let die?

I can argue the point that Liberals are willing to let children and the elderly die. Those who can't defend themselves. Because Liberals are monsters. Because they're cowards. Because they look at an unborn child and see not promise as yet unfulfilled, but rather a cluster of cells, an invader, forcing its way into the tissues of a woman. Want to kill them? Sure, go ahead, they're not alive until they've been born anyway, right? And sometimes not even then.

Likewise, the elderly, who see their medical benefits threatened or outright taken away more every day, because they've got the audacity to live long enough to need them. How many times have I seen west coast Liberal college beasts promoting the idea that any medical help at all should have an age cutoff? I look at these critters and know that in time they'll win, in some places if not all of them, and a horrible part of myself hopes that they live just long enough to need the kind of help that they're going out of their way to make illegal, for no other reason than to see the broken, "Oh, God what did I do?" look on their wretched faces.

I find that the older I get, and the less rational these bastards get, that I have to deal increasingly with anger issues. Don't misunderstand: I'm not a violent person, not in any way. Heck, I've been in exactly one fight in my life, and that was in the seventh grade, a few decades behind me. Yet when I watch what passes for news, and see the talking heads praising the beasts that speak for the brainless and the easily led, I see red. I get so angry that I can't think straight, which is fairly counter productive for someone who wants to make a living with his mind. But how else can I react?

I'm not a big fan of kids. Other than my own, that is, but they walk on water, so what's not to love? On the other hand I find the elderly to be a fount of worthwhile information, and personal reminiscences of the country when it was still worth a damn. Those of us in the middle of these two I'm neither here nor there about (sorry, world). So when I see those in charge promoting things that would make my kids and the elderly become threatened, I cringe.

It had always been my opinion that our single purpose in life is to see to the protection and care of those that can't, or aren't as able, to see to their own. We push back the darkness for one more day, until those that follow can push it back for themselves. To do otherwise is to fail at being human. As such, and I'll be blunt here: Liberals (Socialists, Communists, whatever they call themselves nowadays) are failures at being human beings. At best they are animals. You can quote me on that.

<u>Heating Up</u>
(*The Libertarian Enterprise March 10, 2019*)

It seemed to me, even as a child, that when the Berlin Wall came down that something big had just taken place. As it was explained to me at the time: "The bad guys lost, Harry. The world's seen that Communism doesn't work, that evil doesn't work. We've won." Only we haven't.

For the better part of the last century, the whole of the free world fought, and in the long run defeated, the Red scourge. Out parents, grandparents, aunts and uncles, siblings, children, friends, and neighbors, put their lives on the line, in defense of the world and those that we would leave It to, in open opposition of the boot of tyranny. We pushed back the darkness and made the world safe for democracy. Yet it looks like it's that same democracy that's getting the fires started again.

In the 50's (a decade that I've developed a nostalgia for, even though it was dead and gone two decades before I was hatched) there was a stigma, even a fear, of being identified as a Communist. It's easy to condemn the HUAC, but at the same time I can't point and shout, "Evil men! Shame on you!" Because, even though the charge of Communist was used as a political move as often as not against those that had no Red ties, there were those that were in philosophical revolt against the principles set forth in the Constitution, and for that They could have been lined up against the nearest brick wall and sent off to meet their demonic maker.

My how things have changed. It's not a shameful thing to be identified as a Communist anymore. In many places—I'm looking down my nose at you, New York—it's actually a selling point.

Because I suppose the people that have voted for these "Democratic Socialists" (see: Communists) must have missed fully a century of world history that showed them, in every single instance, that Communism not only doesn't work, but inevitably leads to bloodshed, and the complete loss of individual freedom.

This has been pointed out before, by many more articulate that myself (for these instances see any of the back issues of The Libertarian Enterprise), yet it still falls on deaf ears. Even when the ears aren't deaf, however, the notion that these people are wrong-minded, if not plain evil, is ignored or disregarded. Just in the past few weeks there have been many instances of these media darlings—Nazi Pelosi, Ilhan Omar, Bernie Sanders, and Alexandria Ocasio-Cortez to bemoan a few—have said and done things that would have gotten a Republican tarred and feathered, and yet are not only not shoved under the rug, but openly flouted, knowing as they do that the talking heads that feed us our news will do and say nothing against them.

I saw a meme a few months ago that asked Why Republicans had to stop voting on November 6, but the Democrats could keep going until they won? It's one of those jokes that's funny until it isn't. Because that's the mentality that we're dealing with. A cluster of anti-Americans, about as left leaning as Stalin, only held in check by the Constitution of the United States, going out of their way to remove all that makes us great. To turn us into USSR version 2.0.

A smart person once wrote that the second amendment is so important because it gives you the ability to protect, and insure, the others. When I see these folks talking about stifling, if not outright revoking, the second amendment, my paranoid meter goes off the charts, and I think to myself, "This is the first step in an armed incursion against the law-abiding folks of the United States." The problem is that it's not all that paranoid-sounding anymore, and feels less so all the time.

I've read that paranoids always have a They that they're trying to get away from. A nameless person or group of people that they see as the root of all that troubles them. We don't have a nameless They. We have Pelosi, Oman, Sanders, Ocasio-Cortez, Clinton (pick one), and a plethora of other Communists that would take from us all that we hold dear, and reduce us all to the lowest common denominator. They have no interest in holding all people up to a similar standard; they have a pathological need to hold us all down to one.

Every day I look at the news and wait to hear one of these cretins calling for open revolt. Every night I go to bed amazed that it hasn't happened yet. But I fear that it will, and when that happens this little Cold War that's being fought in the streets and Capitals will warm up fast, with no one left unscathed. Because the road to the future has always been paved in blood. I only hold my breath, waiting to see just what kind of a future that road leads to.

<u>"You Never Have To Give Me Your Money"</u>
(*The Libertarian Enterprise March 17, 2019*)

Profound wisdom can come from the mouths of children. They have this incredible ability to cut through the crap, the constant gray-state of most adult thinking that bogs us down and makes us ineffectual, and get to the core.

Case in point: last year I started listening to The Beatles with my oldest daughter (eight years old at that point, and already leaving her proud daddy choking in her dust). Over a couple of days we listened to just about every Beatles song that I had floating around, and she enjoyed them for the most part, frowning at the occasional acid-induced nonsense. Then, along about three quarters of the way through our marathon, we come across "You Never Give Me Your Money."

We listen to the song, and after a few minutes, she asks me to pause the CD. A few seconds of silence follows said act, and she wonders aloud: "Why should she have to give him her money? Why can't he just earn his own?"

The smile that split my face could have cut my head off.

"Well, honey," I told her (or something similar [I'm hardly as poetic at the time as I like to remember myself afterword]), "She shouldn't. But there are some people out there who think that they're due some of what someone else earns."

More pregnant silence as her mind tried to come to grips with this bit of nonsensical information.

"But that's wrong," she told me.

Over the remainder of that day, and off and on since then, we've discussed the difference between the grace of willfully giving to those left fortunate than yourself, and the wholesale theft that comes from folks who don't want to work for a living. No matter how many different directions she tries to come at it from, the idea of forcing person A to give to person B without the consent of A, because B thinks they deserve it, makes no sense at all to her.

How is it then that a nine year old can see how wrong this is, but that cluster of Liberals in Washington (to say nothing of local Socialists that crop up in regional elections like the weeds they are) can't? I think a lot of it comes down to psychosis.

All kids (excepting the ones that are particularly anti-social [shyly, prepubescent me raises his hand]) are self-serving little psychos. They have to be. It's a survival mechanism. If they don't do what they have to to either lead the pack of slavering animals that most groups of children are, or become a follower/sycophant, they starve out in the cold. But however they fall in the social scheme of things, they all want to be at the top of the heap.

In time they grow out of it. Most of them. They get a sense of their own self worth, and place themselves at the center of a universe of one, until such time as spouses and children shift their orbit and they become human again.

But not all of them grow out of this. We see it all the time, in loudmouthed neighbors, or folks that want to run our towns like gulags, where everyone has to go along with whatever they find most ascetically appealing. At the furthest extreme of that are the politicians.

Power should be reserved for those who don't want it. Especially governmental, regulative, legislative powers. The problem is that those most worthy of power—the ones who won't abuse it because they have no will to use it at all—won't put themselves in a position to assume it. It's a paradox. One that I see no way out of. I'm just not smart enough for it.

I sometimes reread a book by Philip K. Dick call *Solar Lottery,* where leaders are chosen by chance, pure luck. Only it's Dick, so it's never as simple as that. As a mental exercise I wonder how the world would be different—better, worse, or the same—if all public office, to say nothing of other societal services: police, armed forces, trash men, etc., were randomly chosen, for limited, one time terms. A societal draft. It's a moot point as I'm opposed to involuntary servitude of any kind, but as a What If? I find it interesting. Might have to write about that society some day. Could be fun…

It's amazing to me how much talking to my kids makes me think outside the box. How I can excuse many behaviors that my younger self would have found deplorable simply because they've become the norm. We are all numbed by society, by the evils that we see perpetrated every day by the ones that are supposed to be protecting our rights. This is dangerous. More than dangerous, it's suicidal. We need to hold those in power accountable, for their every action, to make sure that they do nothing that we have to explain away to our kids and grandkids. If we can't look at those same children and explain, without feeling like whores in the explaining, why the world is the way it is, then the world is wrong, and we must fix it.

So: No, she doesn't have to give him her money. Neither do we, to fund and progress things that we find offensive, amoral, or Evil. We have every right under heaven to vent our frustrations, and vote those people that are proponents of those things that we find offensive, amoral, and Evil out of office.

To quote a favorite cartoon of mine: They need to be fired. Out of a cannon. Into the sun.

Fools, Damnfools, Willful Idiots, and Monsters
(*The Libertarian Enterprise March 24, 2019*)

Politics is an insane form of lunatic theatre obsessed over, and participated in, by only Fools, damnfools, willful idiots, and monsters. It is a cluster of irrational irrelevancies that all snowball together until such time as the God-given freedoms guaranteed to the citizenry by whatever passes for a Constitution of its given country are finally stripped from them by the very elected officials selected by said willing victims to safeguard them. This inevitably leads to one thing: revolution.

So, given that we have seen this, countless times over the thousands of years of written history, why is it continuing to happen? The incomparable Robert A. Heinlein, amongst others, said that those who don't know the past are doomed to repeat it. Given the sorry state of what passes for history classes in public schools in this country, I can see why this current generation is ignorant of the past, and is therefor rushing headlong into a repeat course of it. Though it doesn't have to be this way. There is still a way to pull their heads out of the sand, to awaken them to the reality of history, one that doesn't begin and end with America as the Evil Empire, and Alexander Hamilton as the only good Founding Father.

Over the course of four years homeschooling my daughters I have gone out of my way to supplement their historical education with readings of *Common Sense, The Decleration of Independence,* and *The Constitution of the United States,* along with whatever other pieces of brilliant history that I can get my greedy little hands on, from McCullough to Stokesburry. Recently we started reading a series of ethical books for children, aimed at raising a freedom-loving generation, touting primarily Libertarian political beliefs in easily digestible fashion. In one such, read just this morning in fact, we were introduced to the works (in an admittedly abbreviated form) of Frederic Bastiat. Amongst the other pearls of wisdom found in the book was this quote: "Life, liberty, and property do not exist because men have made laws. On the contrary, it was the fact that life, liberty, and property existed beforehand that caused men to make laws in the first place."

This being the case, and I can find no reason to disagree with the late Mr. Bastiat on this front, and that our freedoms existed before there were men and women in power to regulate and strip them from us, is it not also the case that the more power we give them, the thicker are the bars of our cells? And why is it that we are so readily able to trust those in power that we more or less agree with, if we so dislike and distrust those that we find unpleasant?   To put it mildly, no one is so trustworthy as to be given free reign with those fundamental rights that give us the ability to thrive.

To use another quote from the late Mr. Bastiat: "If the natural tendencies of mankind are so bad that it is nor safe to permit people to be free, how is it that the tendencies of these organizers are always good?   Do not the legislators and their appointed agents also belong to the human race? Or do they believe that they themselves are made of a finer clay than the rest of mankind?"

And that's what so much of it comes down to, isn't it? A whole political party, who are at the front lines at calling their opponents racist, or sexist, or elitist, or homophobic, who see themselves as so superior, so much greater than, their fellow citizens that they never see us as equals. They see a man, and instantly call him sexist based on nothing more than the fact of his birth, yet would never concede that this instant identification as a predator is in itself sexist. They see a caucasian and instantly decry racism, ignoring the fact that to see race first and react with animosity is in itself an act of racism. They call the Right elitist, ignoring the foundation of their twisted belief system, which is that they know better than we do just what we need.

They are the elite. The same elite that rounded up Jews before and during the second World War. The same elite that ground 20th century Russian history into the bloody snow. They are the elite that would protect your right to abort a baby completely unable to defend itself, but not your right to self defense in the face of overcoming adversity.

I am not elite. Like everyone that I associate with I am a nothing. Just another grunt unimportant in the greater scheme of things, but loved by those who love me and ignored by those that don't. I've never judged a man or woman based on something beyond their control, but will call down heavenly fire on those that consciously act on impulses that I find amoral or evil, regardless of those same things that may be beyond their control. I don't care if you're a man, woman, white, black, gay, or straight. You all have the same worth, or lack thereof, as anyone else in the whole world. But simultaneously I will not cut you any slack based on the color of your skin, or the positioning of your genitals, or who you like to wake up to in the morning, than I would someone in a different position. We're all equal or none of us are, and to look at the world, and see some as having more or less worth than others based on useless data is bigotry, and one that the Democrats flout with impunity because there's no one willing to call them on it that they will ever listen to.

Every time I vote I feel dirty, like I just had to sleep with the landlord to pay the rent. I hate that feeling, and know that in time my children, and theirs, and onward into the immeasurably distant future, will have to have those cold shower moments. And it makes me sick. But it is what it is, and until such time as there are people in office that deserve to be there by doing nothing to rip from their fellow citizens their freedoms, or retain power through fear mongering and hate, those moments will be with us. But that doesn't mean that we have to roll over for the fools, damnfools, willful idiots, or monsters. We can educate our children, show them a better ideal, and pray to God that they have a more successful time making things what they're supposed to be than we have.

(*The Libertarian Enterprise May 12, 2019*)

I'd like to pose a question to you: at what point did we let the government, and the majority that they lord over, have free reign to run our lives, up to and including what we put into our bodies? I have to assume that there are those out there, like myself, who subscribe to Wilson's KYFHO approach to living, but with all of the rolling over for big brother, like the government is actually here to help us, am I truly in the minority when it comes to just being left alone?

As a kid I got all of my pricks and jabs from the local MD, whose offices always looked like some kind of massive family home full of the sick, kept under the watchful eye of a doctor who in retrospect reminds me of no one other than Bob Newhart. Never gave a second thought to it. Just something that everyone was doing, so why question it? After all, if my folks were taking me to get it done, how bad could it possibly be?

I'm not here to rant and rail about vaccinations or anti-vaxxers. Armies on both sides have their reasons for doing, or not doing, whatever they are doing or not doing. Nope, I'm here to ask *why?*

Heinlein had written that there were no examples in history of a time when the majority was right. For the most part I stick by that. Too many folks will naturally bend to the will of the herd. It's a survival mechanism, but one that I feel it's time to break from. Bending to the will of the herd would have removed the inspiration for the American Revolution; would have made us bend knee to the Reds more than fifty years ago. The herd isn't right. It's a globular monstrosity forced upon the people by themselves that will absorb and excrete anything that doesn't fit into the cookie-cutter mold of the greater good. Guess where that leaves individualists, friend? Yep: swirling.

I take personal exception to the idea that the government should have the ability, nay the right, to run our lives. It's all a cyclical problem. Example: government run, socialized health care. The kind that they guilt us over. *Well, who would deny their neighbors, their community, access to health care?* Always make the dissenters villains. The problem comes in afterword. Instead of lifting everyone up to the same high standard that is possible only in a capitalist society, it drags us all down to the same swamp mud level that is the natural environment of all Leftist, collectivist societies. It leads to the government telling us what we can eat (after all, the collective is footing the bill for your bad eating choices now, you heart attack waiting to happen), what you can do (nothing too dangerous), and how you can do it.

It all comes down to control. The more people that are completely reliant on the federal government, the more folks will vote to keep them in power. Gotta keep their slice of the communal pie. No more power to the people; now it's power to the State, and I deny anyone to show me a single example in all of recorded history where that's worked out. What you can eat, what you can do, what you can own. All up to the will of the greater good.

I find it astounding that no one sees the hypocrisy in a government that increasingly insists that everyone get their children vaccinated, regardless or religious or moral exemptions, but will fight tooth and nail for a woman's right to get an abortion. So are we to believe that it is your moral, legal right to remove whatever you want from your body, but the right of the collective to decide what you can and can't have put into it?

There is no consistency in the ideology of the State. Rather, there is only a consistency in their need to control, to micromanage every aspect of your daily lives, at the point of a gun. We are talking about a collective of beasts who have shown again and again that they are ready, willing, and able to fire on and burn alive their own citizens, but are horrified when they look at a president who wants to lock the doors of the border.

I'm not an old man, but I feel increasingly so. I remember being a kid, and seeing things in stark blacks and whites. When I was a surly teenager, they gray state of being started seeping its way into my world view. Things were not as simple as I'd once seen them. It's a stage of development, I suppose, but does it need to be? Because the older I get, the more those grays are washing out, and things are coming into a steadily more black and white focus. There are nowhere near the amount of things that I write up to matters of perspective. Nope: some things are just plain wrong. No perspective, other than a right one and an evil one. Thinking that you have the right to run peoples lives, into the ground more often than not, is an evil perspective.

In many ways the State in necessary evil. Though not in anywhere near the number of ways that those in power seem to think. They are our employees, not our masters, and they have no right to tell us how to live. They need to be reminded that they are not in charge of our lives, and that they just need to keep their hands off. The bureaucracy that infests all forms of government, from local to federal levels, is appalling.   These folks need to be sent packing.

I would call on every able minded individual in the country to force these ideas into the minds of their federal employees, to remind them just what their purpose is. To let them know that if they were in any other form of service industry, they'd have been fired by now.   They are too comfy in their high castles, never afraid enough of the peasants revolting. King George made that mistake once. It cost him a continent. It's only fair that we remind the Powers That Be of this important lesson.

In Praise of Scrooge McDuck
(*The Libertarian Enterprise* May 19, 2019)

I'm going to blame this one on my cousin, Paul Poole.

I become obsessive. I think that's why my wife hates it so much when I bring something new (to me) up to her. Y'see, it means that I'm about to go ape crap in an attempt to get my greedy little hands on everything related to said new thing that I can. It's a lifelong issue. When I was a kid, I was introduced to Heinlein, and spent every cent that I got for the next few years buying all of his books. As a teen, it was Led Zeppelin, and Valiant Comics. Many years, and dollars, later, I still have the LZ records, but very little of the Valiant. Things get traded or sold, to raise funds for the next obsession. It's how I lost all of my Garth Ennis, and gained three shelves worth of Fantastic Four.

A few years ago—closer to a decade than not, and probably on the far side of it—my cousin, the aforementioned Paul D. Pool, suggested the Carl Barks Scrooge McDuck comics, and for the longest time I ignored this suggestion. I've always thought of Disney stuff as inferior, to be honest. They've let out very few movies during my lifetime that I could even stand to sit through once, let alone multiple times. Their many so-called contemporary classic (I'm looking at you, *Lion King!*) are, to me, completely unwatchable.   To call them garbage would be an insult to the refuse that I bring out to my garbage man every Friday morning. The trash at least served a purpose at one time.

Then, a short while ago, I stumbled across a few of the books of The Carl Barks Library at my own local library, and decided to give them a shot. Dislike

Disney as I do, I will be honest and admit that I have some fond memories of the *Ducktales* cartoon from the 80's. In the spirit of that nostalgia, I picked up one of the books.

Lemme tell ya, folks: I'm very glad I did.

Aside from the incredible artwork and storytelling, what we have in Scrooge is an honest capitalist—in fact, one who is unapologetically so—who worked for every cent he has, and has zero time for freeloaders. There are no handouts, but at the same time, he prides himself on being square. For those of us who've read the stories, you know that bit: Smarter than the smarties, tougher than the toughies…

In modern America—I'd say "On modern earth," but the rest of the world has always hated capitalists, so screw 'em—folks are too ready to look at someone with money, and instantly see the fat cat, the thief, the one who got where they are on the backs of the little guy. While I'm sure that there are many (I've worked for a few of the pigs myself) who make it by any means necessary up to and including intentionally sticking it to the little guy, there are also those few with the intelligence, the integrity, and the grit to grab a job by the neck and get it done. The ones who earn every cent through blood, sweat, and tears. To drop the leaches in with the Atlases is sickening. It's also discrimination, prejudice, and exactly the thing that Liberals and other Communists are supposed to be fighting against. By why stand on integrity from parasites that haven't got any?

In modern media there are next to no role models for younger folks to look up to. Everyone (even in children's programming and literature) is miserable, or shady in the extreme, heroes only when compared with the villains. While that works great for those of us who are fans of Judge Dredd, it's not the kind of thing that we want our kids reading.

What is humanity's problem with heroes? Time was they were something to aspire to, even if your grasp will never be far enough. Now they're a source of scorn. The boy scout mentality is a thing of the past. Superman is dead. It's just not right.

Though I refuse to let these things lie, to look back on a past that I remember as better than the here and now, because it's not the past that my children have to live in, but a future that come hell or high water will be golden. We need to promote the idea to those that follow us that honor, integrity, heroism aren't just lost ideals, that they're alive and well in all of them. We need to teach them to stand up, to look the buggers in the face, and say, "Not today, thanks."

But, I wander. My mind gets off on these tangents, rants on about things that I'm told don't matter, when I know down in my marrow that they do. I'm far from perfect. I'm lazier than is good for me, and I hold grudges like they're life preservers. I need to work on these. I look at my children and see an inspiration, to not just continue with the status quo, but to aim for more. To be the kind of upstanding bugger that they need me to be. I'm never going to be rich, and I'm getting too old to be an adventurer, but that doesn't matter. For my kids I can be anything they need me to be.

Philosophical meanderings aside, I do owe a word of thanks to my cousin for insisting a decade or more ago that I give these little stories a shot. They've entertained me, and more, they've entertained a ten year old girl who still looks up to me like I'm cool. It won't be long before she sees through the golden armor that she imagines I wear and sees the nerdy little man that I am. Until that day, though, I will be what I can, and will do what I can, and will share in adventures with her, even if by proxy, following around a cartoon duck.

*2022 update: Disney still sucks.

<u>Why Do Vampires Suck?</u>
(*The Libertarian Enterprise May 26, 2019*)

I used to be a big fan of zombie books and movies. In the golden age of the 80's, when they were still hard to find, and the ones that you did manage to get your hands on were still interesting. Sure, they almost exclusively payed homage to Romero's *Night of the Living Dead,* but they at least went about it their own way. John Skipp and Craig Spector's *Book of the Dead* comes immediately to mind. An incredible collection, it introduced me to such diverse talents as Joe R. Lansdale, David J. Schow, and Robert McCammon. And while it's true that their follow-ups to this anthology never came close to reaching the greatness of the first, if they'd done nothing else with their careers than *BotD*, their place in genre fiction would have been cemented.

After this things get muggy, however. Since the mid- to late-80's, zombies have been everywhere, proliferating books, movies, and television shows with mundane gorefests that are nothing more than a less enjoyable rehashing of all that's come before. Now, don't get me wrong, there have been some examples of good zombie stuff over the years—*Shaun of the Dead, Re-Animator,* J. L. Bourne's *Day by Day Armageddon* series—but they are so few and far between that they stand out like mountain peaks amidst the mediocrity of clouds that is the rest of the slop.

I enjoy horror stories, I'll admit. Some of them, anyway. I like the stuff that gets behind the eyes and moves in. The stuff that takes root and makes you loose sleep for a few days. Now I don't mean gore. Any fool can produce gore, and most folks seem to think that blood and viscera equals horror, and they're wrong. Which isn't to say that good horror doesn't have any of the red stuff in it, it can. What separates good horror from the everyday is the creators ability to use that gore to hit at something deeper. Something that you can't just wash off.

The last few years have been real disappointments for me in regards to horror in general. In truth, though, I can say the same thing about nearly every genre out there. For every Dean Koontz, there's a dozen Stephen Kings; for every F. Paul Wilson, there's two dozen Dan Brown's. Add to this the losses over the last couple years of Harlan Ellison, Charles L. Grant, Tom Clancy, and other worthwhile creators and things are just bleak. Genre fiction is dying, amalgamating until everything is the same as everything else, and all that's left worth reading or watching or listening to are those same peaks. Thank God for folks like Koontz, Wilson, Schow, Michael Connelly, Robert Crais, McCullough, and those sainted genre folks who write for TLE.

In general, I lean more toward reprint publishers. True, in many cases they are more expensive than others, but at least they print things worth looking at. If not for the smaller houses like Haffner and Nightshade, I'd have precious little to read. I'd have to troll used book stores (not that I don't, already) for Hammilton, Laumer, and other greats. I guess that's why, when I find something new that's worth reading I grab onto it like a life preserver. Which brings us to *Sweeter Than Wine,* by L. Neil Smith.

I'm less of a fan of vampire fiction than I was of the zombie variety. I was never a fan of Dracula (though there've been quite a few worthy flicks based on the over rated novel), and after my brief obsession with Anne Rice, never bothered to look back at her hyper-effeminate blood suckers (though, in truth, *Queen of the Damned* is still a solid book). I will give King his due for *Salem's Lot,* but the sparkly *Twilight* vamps were worthless to me from the start, and every one of the teen vampire TV shows was dead on arrival.

Of the many vampire short stories and novels that I've read, there were only a handful that stood out to me. There is the classic *I Am Legend*, by Richard Matheson, who, near as I can tell, never wrote a bad word. There's your high water mark. Close on its heals is *The Light at the End,* by *Book of the Dead*'s own Skipp and Spector, a nice little 80's-era brick that I sat down and read over a weekend, finding myself completely unable to put it down. Looking at the pulps, we have wonders like Hamilton's *The Vampire Master,* and anything Seabury Quinn wrote on the subject. Likewise anything that Charles Grant graced us with. On the shorter side of this list would be Schow's "Last Call For The Sons of Shock," which set my Universal Monster fanboy mind working on overdrive, and Wilson's "Midnight Mass," which counts among one of the finest short stories that I've ever read. I'm sure that there have been others that I enjoyed, but these are the ones that stand out in my mind. The ones against which all other vampire fiction is judged.

So then, after a long route, where does this put Mr. Smith's *Sweeter Than Wine*? I'm not going to be the sycophant here and lie, saying that it's on the scale of Matheson, as nothing is. Nor is it over-the-top insane like *The Light at the End.* What it is is a competent, well written little story that I found myself enjoying, despite the obvious fact that this isn't Smith's genre of choice. What it has going for it is what his work always has going for it.   Namely characters, political jabs, and a Libertarian worldview that permeates the page.   It is closer to mainstream than any of his other work, and as such if it were five times longer and less individualistic would offer him his best chance at headlining fame.

Its length might be its only actual drawback, as I finished it up and wanted more. Full disclosure: when this book was first published, way back in 2011, I skipped it, mostly due to the aforementioned avoidance of most vampire stuff. In a way I'm glad that I skipped it. Not because it wasn't worth reading, because it most certainly was that, but because with a new book coming at us later this year, I won't have to wait eight years for a follow-up. I just have to be patient.

Given how he's handled the vampire genre, I'd offer the challenge to L. Neil to see what other classic monsters he could tackle. A werewolf story might be too similar, especially given that the hairy buggers are explained over the course of this book. Maybe a Frankenstein story, as it's much more science fiction in nature than horror anyway. Though a mummy adventure would be fun, as well. Oh, well. It's a moot point any rate, but a fun exercise.

The New Racism

(The Libertarian Enterprise June 16, 2019)

Yesterday I was physically sickened reading the words of Kristen Gillibrand, who compared being pro-life to being racist.   Besides the overwhelming idiocy of this sub-human would-be baby-killer, I think what shocked me more was the lack of shock that I felt.   This kind of anti-life monstrousness is nothing new, but has become over the last few months the rallying cry for the political Left in America.

I wrote a few months back that one of the primary differences between the Left and the Right is who they are willing to kill or let die. I'd argued that the Right was willing to send those folks between 18 and 65—y'know: *adults*—off to meet their maker, while the Left would much rather aim their genocidal lunacies at children and the elderly. I have always assumed that they aim at these two specific groups because they were (generally) less able to fight back than the 18 to 65 year olds. Damn it all, I hate being proven right.

I'm going to get in trouble for this, but I'll let it out and screw the consequences: I am opposed to abortion.   It is not because I am, as the creature called Gillibrand would attest, a racist.   Nor an I opposed to abortion because I feel that women are some kind of property, with no right to regulate their own bodies.   If being pro-life is akin to being anti-woman then there are millions of intelligent, strong, educated women that are anti-woman as well, and I call crap on that.   I am anti-abortion, pro-life, whatever you want to call it, because I see it as the sole responsibility of human adults to see to the safe upbringing, education, and protection of children. Regardless of age or whether or not they're outside the body of their mothers or not. I was ruined at an early age by Dr. Seuss. I firmly believe that a person is a person, no matter how small.

I admit that I find it sadly amusing that these same pro-choice politicians and celebrities (whose opinions are about as worthwhile as the refuse that I threw in the trash after breakfast this morning) are the political successors—if not the original offenders, like a certain less-than-human recent Presidential candidate—who would spit in the faces of returning troopers in the 60's and 70's, calling them baby-killers, and assaulting them with signs all in the name of peace. The irony of this, that they themselves would become the ones to stand on the platform of pro-choice, is not lost on me. The animalistic aspects of these selfsame non-humans as they promote the action of exposing a child to allow it do die, or allowing late-term abortion is not lost on me either.

Quite a number of years ago, Dr. Johnson wrote that the person who makes a beast of himself gets rid of the pain of being a man. He may as well have been writing about the frontrunners and soulless figureheads of the modern Democratic and Democratic Socialist parties. Because these cretins are not humans anymore. They've gotten rid of that pain. They've embraced all things bad and anti-human, and a warm seat in waiting for them in hell.

So, by contemporary standards, my being anti-abortion, anti-socialist, pro-gun, pro-constitution, pro-personal responsibility, makes me sexist, racist, whatever other kind of -ist that you can name, and if that's what they call being moral these days then so be it. So are most of my family and friends, regardless of race, gender, or anything else that doesn't matter in the long run. But let it be known that I've never judged someone by how they look, but on how they feel. All people may be created equal, but some people aren't people anymore. They're the animals that are more equal than others, and we as a country have never looked kindly at those who positioned themselves higher than us. If it's not earned, then it's worthless. And they're worthless.

<u>**Leaving the House**</u>
(The Libertarian Enterprise June 23, 2019)

It's funny to me to see how the media are losing their minds—to say nothing of blowing something out of proportion (they've never done *that* before)—over a couple of Trump supporters declaring that The Donald should have more than two terms in office. Another fascist, right-wing grab for totalitarian power, I suppose.   Inevitably the comparisons to the Nazis, but never to the equally blood thirsty Soviets, whom they idolize. (I'd like to hear them describe what they see as "Right Wing," and tell me how the Nazis were right wing. Just more lefty statist monsters.)

A few years back, when clearly half the country told the powers that be that they were sick and tired of political business as usual and the parasitic socialists that grab onto it, there were countless calls of sexism and stolen elections. Fifty percent of all those who voted were branded white supremacists and chauvinists.   Calls for impeachment were thrown out instantly, along with charges of treason and collusion.   Many states suggested a change to the electoral college because it didn't serve them as they felt it should. There was a great weeping and gnashing of teeth.   We were shown proof positive that it was not the system that was broken, but rather the cretins that festered in it.

Though I may well be proven wrong, I think that President Trump has the next election in the bag. His victory will be by a significant margin, and that will make what little grip the Never-Trumpers have on reality completely disappear. They will call for blood, all in the name of what they see as equality and the failed American dream, and the progressives and socialists and communists will foam at their filthy little mouths. Damnfools in California and New York and other likeminded places will look to a coming revolution, reveling in the prospect of ending the lives of Americans they disagree with. They will set the bonfires upon which they would cremate all of our hard won freedoms.

They won't win, whether it comes to a shooting war or not. They can't. Simply because they stand for nothing more than ripping down what better men have built. Because the rest of us, the sane ones who know that there are problems but that those same problems can't be defeated by destroying the human will, are better people, in every regard. We don't look for the fight, but once it's brought, we fight it, with our blood, sweat, and tears. And we win. Because that's what we do.

In less than six years, after his second term in office, Donald Trump will leave the White House. Some will cheer his leaving, others will mourn it. After he's gone off to whatever he opts to do next, there will still be those who will do their best to bring him down and make his presidency impotent in the eyes of history. It is to history that they should look. In the end they'll be footnotes, if that. Schumer and Booker and Pelosi and the ever despicable, drooling moron AOC and all the rest of the also-rans will be forgotten. They should be. Their whole claim to fame (or infamy) is their ability to breed discontent. To the ash pile with them.

I worry about the world that I leave to my children. I think all parents do to some extent. It's a survival mechanism. For our lines to continue, our kids have to have a world to thrive in. What they have to look forward to I don't know, though I suspect it'll be more of the same, with the liberty-minded and the fascists (democrats, in case you were wondering who I was talking about) flip-flopping on each other, those in power being those least worthy, and headaches agogo. What I don't see them having to worry about is some phantom right-wing dictator, a president for life. Generally speaking, we're just not built that way. We leave that for the other side.

*2022 update: It is amazing to me, frankly, just how depraved and villainous the other side has proven themselves to be over the last 18 months.

<u>Hello, Leave Me Alone, Thanks</u>

(The Libertarian Enterprise July 7, 2019)

When did the idea of minding your own business fall so out of fashion as to be contrary to modern sensibilities? I remember asking my folks many times as a youngster "What's wrong with that little crying brat over there?" only to have them tell me it was none of my business. As long as the crying brat in question wasn't weeping because mom or dad had been viciously beating them, whatever was the matter was no matter of mine. Nor was it the problem of any odd passerby who happened to see me crying when I was having a fit of my own. Sink or swim, it was all on ya, have a nice day, don't let the door split you on the way out.

All that common courtesy and kind hearted uncaring has gone by the wayside, it seems, in favor of a nanny state, where everyone's business is everyone else's, and woe to the person who just doesn't want to be bothered. Why does it have to be this way though? What has brought us to this increasingly hive minded point? Could it be the endless intrusiveness of modern technology and celebrity obsession? Could it be that you don't have to even go out of doors any more to be a stalker? Everything is right there, at the finger tips. What's worse: you don't even have to geek it out anymore, spending who knows how many hours or days hiding in bushes, waiting for the best shot. Nope, the talking heads that tell us how to think and feel and act and vote are doing it all for us, with 24 hour live streams of their lives and embarrassments, until we're so full of useless knowledge about the never rans that we hardly know who we are anymore.

Is it that we're so afraid of being alone, or terrified of the responsibility to take care of our own needs, that we're ready to saddle up to the nearest hitching post and let ourselves rot there? (I'll admit that I know next to nothing about horses, so if that last bit of rant makes no sense I apologize. Too much of a city boy, I guess.)

There was a point in time, not even that long ago in the celestial scheme of things, when folks—that'd be men and women, don't want anyone to think I'm being noninclusive—were ready, willing and able to go about life on their own terms. There were people that would trek out into areas of the world completely unknown to civilization and settle down, making a life or a fresh grave for themselves. They'd hunt and gather and build and reproduce and make that place theirs if it was at all possible. I guess it was a "Can-do," a bit of grit that is portrayed to modern young humans as something archaic, if not downright racist, but then what isn't these days?

It's all paled compared to what it used to be. Individuals are presented as (repeating myself) racist, sexist, transphobic, anti-worker, whatever else the week kneed Leftist cretins feel like calling them because they can't find a legitimate argument for their way of life other than "Well, I'm too much of a milquetoast liberal snowflake to survive in that kind of environment, so it must be evil!" People who want nothing from their neighbors other than to be treated as human beings, and otherwise to be left alone, are touted as being antisocial and dangerously violent. I suppose there could be a glint of truth in that one, as who wouldn't be violent if their busybody neighbors and their federal friends raided their homes, opened fire on their spouses and offspring, and effectively executed them for not wanting to be bothered?

I'm an individual. Fairly antisocial, too, truth be told. I bother with folks when I want to, in situations of my choosing, and for the duration that I'm willing to suffer through it. There are times when I have to be nice to head cases that I'd much rather walk away from: at work, when I'm being paid to be nice to head cases, rather than walk away from them. As long as I don't see or suspect you of beating on your spouse or children, I don't really care what you're doing. MYOB, all the way, insofar as your business doesn't get in the way of me doing mine. So that being the case, I'd be very appreciative if the rest of the world would KYFHO while I'm MYOB, and if my lack of caring bothers you, I'd have to ask (smile on face and twinkle in eye): DILLIGAF?

I hate those little quips about there being two kinds of people in the world. While some can be pretty funny, most are just pretentious and annoying. But it does seem to me that there are two kinds of people in the world: those who need to be in control of everything you do, and those who just want to be left alone. Live and let live, have a great day, and get the hell off my lawn. The world would be a much better place, I think, if there were more of the latter, and next to none of the former.

So, as you go out this week (when you read this, or at least skim it, the 4th of July is past, but as I sit here writing it it's still a day away) be good human beings. Leave folks alone. Mind your own business, until someone makes their business yours. Bring this isolationist, nonconformist mentality with you into whatever your future holds. Remember that you aren't owed any part of what your neighbor's earned, any more than they've earned the sweat from your own brow. Keep your head down, and don't start anything that earns you a kick in the pants. And be able to keep those times when you've had to get violent low enough to be counted on four fingers, keeping the middle one free to share with those folks that you gave a pass, even when they deserved nothing more than a pop in the teeth.

<u>**A Plead to Bleed**</u>

(*The Libertarian Enterprise July 14, 2019*)

Nothing political this time. At least I don't think so. Y'never know, though, do you?

What I'd like to blather about this week is reading. And writing, I suppose. But mostly reading. See, when I was a kid my uncle started in on the brainwashing, dropping writers like Heinlein, Asimov, Pournelle, and their like on me. As I got older, so did the subject matter. This is where L. Neil, Koman, Pournelle *with* Niven (still the only collaborative duo that wrote above their already incredible solo standard when working together) and a couple of others. Like so many folks before me, I was dropped down a rabbit hole that I never have fully emerged from. Not that I'd want to.

I spent more years than I care to look back on reading and rereading the same dozen or so folks. Oh, there'd be brief times when I'd "Discover" someone new and devour their stuff, but in the end it was always the same people, drawing me back in, like friends or family. These stories were a mythology, these characters things from heroic tradition. I was always in good hands.

But here's the problem: Most of the folks that shaped my mind at so formative a time are gone now. Heck, most of them were gone by the time I'd started reading them. If memory serves, I'd started in on Heinlein in '89 or so, a year after his passing. Same with L'Amour. I was probably 13 when I started reading Asimov, and I'm fairly sure he was either gone by then, or on his way out. Niven and Pournelle stuck around—until Jerry died a bit ago— but their work together was few and far between, and Pournelle's own solo output was never voluminous to start with. There were endless stories from Bradbury and Ellison, but even these dwindled by the time they met their maker, not that any of my local bookshops bothered to cary their stuff anyway. Likewise when I'd asked them to get in copies of missing books by J. Neil Schulman (whose *Alongside Night* I didn't read until I was an adult, because I just couldn't get the thing), or Victor Koman, whose books are so persona non grata that even my local library refuses to handle them. (I've asked them why on numerous occasions, but with no success; I gather that it's not the decision of the librarians, themselves, but rather the over arching powers that be who want, above all else, to not offend the SJW's.)

It really comes home for me that most of the writers that impacted me in my youth are gone. Most especially when I sit down to read with my kids. That's what has kicked up all this dust in my mind.

Recently I started reading Asimov's *I, Robot* to my girls. While surrounded by people who find robots to be anything from creepy to evil to downright demonic, my oldest hears Isaac's words and her eyes light up. She wants to hear the stories. More, she needs to. I remember the feeling. That indefinable *need* to know what happens next, to the exclusion of all else. I envy them this time. I remember the first time I read "Robbie," and that sense of wonder and awe at a story well-told can never be recaptured. The best we can hope for is to live it again by proxy through the eyes of our kids.

So then, to the question at the core of this short article: Who will they read?

As an adult, as I've stated already, I read mostly the same people that I read earlier in life. The same ones that my family read earlier in their lives. Is this to be the way of things? Has the medium of storytelling fallen so low that by the time my own kids are adults, reading to their own kids, that the best they can hope for is 80-100 year old science fiction stories written before their old man was born? True, there are still L. Neil, J. Neil, Koman, Koontz, Mike Baron, Sarah Hoyt, F. Paul Wilson, Chuck Dixon, and Graham Nolan (Yes, I'm name-dropping, but for a reason: if you don't already read them, *remedy that!*), but they're only a few people. We need more.

I write. Every nerd does, I think, whether it's fan fiction or blogs or whatever. I write short novels and stories. They're not great, but I like them. I wish to God that I could write something that someone could read, and say in later years that it was their favorite book. I don't think I ever will. Not enough talent, not enough smarts. But I try my best. You can, too. I truly feel that everyone has at least one story in them. One thing that is distinctly their own. It could be a twenty word anecdote, or a thousand page opus. Doesn't matter. Write. Create. Pour out your life's blood onto the page. Leave it all out there on the street, with no shyness or regrets. It might not be great, but then again it might. So, create, for the sake of those that follow, as much for your own sake. Give them something to read that doesn't suck. Remind them that there are still storytellers worth reading out there. Please, I'm begging you, not just for my kids and their kids, but for myself. Because sometimes it just feels too dark out there.

<u>**Two Symptoms of a Greater Sickness**</u>
(*The Libertarian Enterprise July 21, 2019*)

I'm not sure just how this is going to work out, so bear with me…

It seems to me that there is an ever-growing sickness in the United States today, one perfectly exemplified by two seemingly unrelated, ongoing incidents. I'm sure that there are countless others, but for me (at least lately) these are the ones that've grabbed my mind, and won't let go, for various reasons.

First is the constant comparisons from the brainless political fanatics on the left that call themselves Democrats or Democratic Socialists, (without ever having the grit to come out and really laying it on the line by saying what they are: Communists), between the refuge camps and the Holocaust. It would be all too easy to see this lapse in sanity as a condemnation of the public school system that must so downplay the horrors of the Holocaust that these hardly multi-celled proto-Cromags can look at what is happening to legally detained illegal immigrants and see anything near the sickening anti-humanity that was perpetrated by the Nazis before and during the second World War. Don't misunderstand: nearly any death is a regrettable one, and the deaths of children are always appalling—irony of this being that the pieces of pinko shit calling "Foul!" at the border because of the deaths of kids are the same ones who say it is a woman's right to abort an unwanted child, practically up to the point when it emerges from said mother naturally—but to say that 24 children dying in ICE custody is on the same scale as literally MILLIONS (I want those bastards in Congress who think this comparison is applicable to sound out that word and look it up, as obviously schooling in general, and *counting* in particular, was never their strong suit) of victims of Nazi Socialism is barbaric in the extreme, and such an affront to what passes for humanity in the rest of us that the best thing they can do for the world and themselves is to just end it all, and spare us their hateful, nonsensical, anti-human, idiocies.

Wow. That felt good to get that off my chest. Heavy stuff for me, as I usually blather on about non-issues, because for the most part I try not to let things get under my skin. But these sons of bitches get to me, in ways that I never understood as a kid. With adulthood comes a semblance of understanding, and with that understanding comes a fury directed toward Evil (notice the capital 'E') that tells us that nothing is wrong, that all things are subject. The kind of Evil that says to disagree with Socialism is to be racist, sexist, transphobic, and whatever other nonsense they can cobble together to make us shut up. Well, sorry to break it to you you knuckle-dragging garbage scows, but people are fed up with being shut up. We are all ready, willing, and Goddamned ABLE to stand up for ourselves, so, for what it's worth: bring it, bub.

Onto the second track: the apparent oncoming attack on Area 51. I'm sorry, what?

So, nearly a million people, as I write this, are actively preparing to attack Area 51, famous (supposed) warehouse of all things UFO and EBE related. Okay. Let me get this straight: a group of violent insurgents is not only going to attack a US military base, but has gone on to tell said base when they're going to do it, and just how many of them are supposed to be there. Wow. Y'know what: go ahead. I'd love to watch on the news as this cluster of morons runs at the base (or drives, I guess, assuming they can remember how to do so); to see their cars and themselves get blown to bits on the landmines that I have little doubt are there; to see those that are left get cut to ribbons by the waiting armed forces stationed there, to say nothing of those flow in just for the occasion. Remember, they protect from enemies foreign and *domestic*, pal, and if you're attacking the base make no mistake: that means you. In the back of my mind I see the sand turned red with the blood of nearly one million (undoubtedly) Democrat/Socialist/Communist invaders, the few left crawling their way out under a barrage of fire, while the ghost of R. Lee Ermey rides down on a chariot from Heaven to rip off their balls, so they cannot contaminate the rest of the world.

So: what do these two things have to do with each other? They're symptoms of a growing sickness In America. A sickness of idiocy, where the loudest voice, no matter how moronic (AOC), is the call of the day. And it is figureheaded by those four sexist, racist, religionist congresswomen that seem to thing themselves untouchable. They call their own Speaker racist because she calls them out on being pieces of shit. Never thought I'd agree with Nancy Pelosi, but there it is. Pelosi is called racist because she is a white female who dares stand against them. They call President Trump racist and sexist and anything else you can think of because he is a heterosexual white male. That they disagree with what he says and does is secondary. God help them if they are ever called the garbage that they are by a non-binary, Muslim minority. Their revolving hate machine might go crazy like Robbie the Robot at the end of Forbidden Planet. Might be worth

looking at, though.   If things keep going in the
direction they are, we all might just get to see.

The Bright Side of a Situation That Never Had One

(The Libertarian Enterprise July 28, 2019)

I'm in the early stages of a new story (book? Not sure. We'll see), and part of that research is looking into early Soviet history. This has led me to consider a number of books (note: if you happen to know of any particularly good, though not too cumbersome, volumes, let me know: I'm on Facebook and Mewe), each one of which I did a bit of looking into. More the writers than the books at first. I didn't want to saddle myself up with some kind of Communist apologist monologue that in any way attempts to make the Reds look like anything other than they were: an evil menace. When the late Ronald Reagan called them "The Evil Empire," he spoke arguably the greatest truth even uttered by a President, and a breath of fresh air after the placating, "Please don't nuke us" ridiculousness of his immediate predecessor. To try to make this Evil Empire look like anti-heroes or, worse, protagonists in the story of civilization, is unforgivable.

Which leads us to my problem this week. Looking into one book in particular (I'm still going through it at the moment, so I'll hold off on recommending or even naming it until such time as I don't feel like I'm wasting your time and mine) I was shocked, then sickened, to see not one but many reviewers calling the writer to task because he showed a very one-sided, anti-Communist, anti-Stalin version of Soviet history. Why dwell on the "Few things" that the Communists and Uncle Joe did wrong, they asked, when society could be much better served by exemplifying what they did right?

I'm sorry: what?

One brain donor spouting such words I could almost write up to random stupidity. But many, making the same argument? I hate to say it folks, but it looks more and more like the brainwashing of the youth of America is well under way, and in no time at all people will be saying, outright and with great sadness, that the wrong side won the Cold War.

So, for those out there (not you, gentle reader, who are intelligent and well read in history and many other subjects) who think that the Soviet Union generally, and Uncle Joe Stalin specifically, were antiheroes, or misunderstood, or were the unsung but ultimately defeated heroes of the decades-long Cold War, let me give you a very brief lecture about just how dribbling stupid you are.

To start with Joe Stalin, that arguably most recognized late leader of the former Evil Empire, was anything but a hero of the unwashed masses. Quite the contrary, he was responsible for the murders of millions—read that again: *millions!*—of human beings, somewhere between 40 and 60 million by what I've been able to gather. To say that this monster (not a man; anyone capable of doing what he did has given up his right to be counted among the rest of us human beings) is heroic in any way is to condone the murders of millions of people, and at the risk of making enemies that I'd rather not have as friends anyway, if you are the kind of *thing* capable of condoning these atrocities then you are a monster as well, and to hell with you. To quote the beast: "A single death is a tragedy; a million deaths is a statistic."

This is to say nothing of the indescribable evils perpetrated by the Soviets against every territory that they occupied, the additional murders of countless men, women, and children, as well as the systematic rape of women and children, something so sickening that if you can still look at their history and think them as AT ALL noble or worthwhile you should do the world a favor and just kill yourself. Seriously. If you can know, beyond doubt, that you're rooting for a murder machine capable of sexually assaulting CHILDREN you have no business in my world. You should die, have your bodies cremated, and those ashes shot into space, so as to not contaminate the world with even a particle of your wretched presence.

Understand something: these were no heroes. These were beasts. Subhuman. Animals, only worse. If you think that there's something wrong with dwelling on the "Few things" that they did wrong, you're sick. If you think that society could be much better served by exemplifying what they did right you have no place in civil society. Not to mince words: you're garbage. Filth. A murderer in thought if not action. There is no bright spot to the Soviet monster, and if you think for even a single goddamned second that there was, you can rot in hell, right next to good ol' Uncle Joe.

*2022 update: my opinion of Communism, and Communists, has if anything, become over the years. To Hades with them.

<u>**Speaking Up**</u>
(*The Libertarian Enterprise Sep. 15, 2019*)

I have to wonder some times if the frontrunners on the Left are actively pushing for a bloodbath.   There can be no other explanation for their constant attacks on Bill of Rights advocates.   I can see no other sane reason why they would constantly be calling for what the esteemed El Neil calls Victim Disarmament in the wake of shootings carried out by lunatics who wouldn't abide by any law they pass in the first place.   Do they want us dead? Is that what they're really up to?

I saw in passing on Glen Beck's *The Blaze* Facebook page a commentator asking if liberals were actually, all joking aside, Evil (notice the capital 'E'). I've wondered the same thing myself, more than once.   There is ample evidence of it, after all. They're willing to let us die to achieve their Red scheme.   We've seen that time and again.   They're willing to grind us under their jackboot to make the world over in the image of their gods (here see Stalin, Lenin, and of the plethora of vile monsters whose passing and failure the Left mourn and lament daily). As has been seen I don't know how many times, they're willing to fight to sustain the life potentially contained within an egg (as long as it's an animal egg), but will fight just as viciously to make sure an unborn human child dies, should the parents see fit to murder it.   So, yes, speaking objectively, and as someone who does believe in the existence of Evil, in its purest form, not as an abstraction or theological might-be, I can see no other more appropriately descriptive word to sum them up other than Evil.

With their constant calls of racist or sexist or transphobic   or whatever other hatchet word they blurt out like so much hot air at anyone and everyone who calls them on their hypocrisy, we've finally gotten to a point where there's not even a shred of sanity left in them. They've joined the agenda of blood, and nothing short of the total obliteration of their opponents will ever do. For years, at least as far back as that honestly over rated anti-human H.G. Wells, there have been calls to cull the human race into a more manageable number. Manageable in what way I leave to the reader's imagination. Recently we have that pinko beast Sanders calling for the use of American currency to aid in abortion in foreign countries, to help the world and push back the fictional ravages of global warming. Love the world, kill your baby. And people cheer.

They...*CHEER...*

There was a time when I'd argued that while the Liberal talking heads were inhumane garbage, nevertheless the average, walkin' around town Lefty was basically a decent, if politically wrong minded, person. Yet after seeing those self same average, walkin' around town Liberals shout their heads off enthusiastically when their preferred candidates are actively pushing for the murder of God only knows how many unborn children, I concede that I must change that opinion. They're not good folks who are misguided. They're just as bad as their goose stepping overlords and masters.

My lovely and understanding (and admittedly smarter then I) wife has asked me on many occasions of late why I interact with folks fairly often in regards to politics. It makes me unhappy, makes me say things in a more harsh way than I otherwise would, and frankly makes me cuss up a storm, a bad habit that I'd gotten largely out of for years. So, why?

Why jump into something that makes me miserable? It all comes down to something I read years ago.

I'm sure most of you've heard this already. Though this is only paraphrasing, it went something like, First they came for the Jews, but I was no Jew so I said nothing. It goes on from there, ending pointedly with, Then they came for me, and there was no one left to speak for me. So that's why. That's why I just can't keep my mouth shut. Why so many of those whose opinions hold so much weight with me can't keep their mouths shut. Because there will inevitably come a time, if we don't speak up now, that they will come for us, and no one will be left to speak for us.

We push back so that we might avoid shooting back. So, if applicable or not, repeat after me:

They came for the gun owners, and whether or not I
was one I spoke up;
They came for the unborn children, and whether or
not I had one I spoke up;
They came for our property, and whether or not I
owned any I spoke up;
They came for our lives, and whether or not I liked
mine I spoke up;
They came for our freedoms, and whether or not we
use them , we spoke up.

Amen, and God bless.

(The Libertarian Enterprise Oct. 13, 2019)

I was walking into work a few weeks back, minding my own business, when I was shouted at in the parking lot by three total strangers. They called me a racist, asked me what the hell my problem was, and made generally menacing gestures toward me. What was I doing to make them so mad? I was walking in with a copy of William L. Shirer's *The Rise and Fall of the Third Reich: A History of Nazi Germany* under my arm.

As I'm sure many of the folks reading this wonderful magazine already know, the cover of every edition of Shirer's "little" book that I've ever seen is a solid black, with a swastika front and center. It's perfect in its eye-catching presentation, and leaves no doubt in the mind of the reader that this book is going to be something heavy, not only in sheer weight (1,000 + page books have that) but also in emotional impact. I read it 20 years ago as a teenager, and felt the need to go through it again.

So, there I am, walking through the parking lot of my place of employment, on my way to begin my work day, my lunch break reading tucked under my arm, when these three people start yelling at me. Safely across the parking lot, they call me names and throw angry looks at me. I give them a quick look over—granola munching post-hippy hippy chick, bitch-bun-wearing hipster, and socks and sandals, sharp-bearded millennial, each early to mid 20's, each at first glance completely worthless—and go on my way.

Still, I grit me teeth. They yelled at me. Not because I was doing anything particularly wrong. Not because I was dressed in an offensive way (dad shorts and a t-shirt). Nope, but because they saw me walk into a store, reading something with a swastika on the cover. Knee-jerk hate. Instantly triggered. Fascism loves a lack of historical perspective.

I read a lot of history. American history mostly, and that of other countries insofar as it overlaps with that of the US. As such, I've read about 20th century Russia, the Mexican-American War, and Nazi Germany. I've devoured the works of David McCullough and Shelby Foote among many others. In researching EVIL people to better write them, I've read The *Communist Manifesto*, *Mein Kampf*, and the works of Lenin. My local library has sought out many obscure bits of anti-human ramblings to give me a better glimpse into the twisted psyches of mad men and monsters. (Though the board of directors still blatantly refuses to order in or even accept free copies of the writings of SEK3. Too controversial, I suppose.) The Communists and Nazis are perfect examples of just why we fight against those that would destroy us, should they gain too much—or any—power.

I've got relatives who have walked into our home and seen Shirer's book on my shelves and asked me to either turn it around so as to not display the swastika on the spine in their presence or flat out demand that I throw the book out. Personal note: it still has its place on my shelves, regardless of how uncomfortable its being there makes people. They don't care that it isn't a Nazi propaganda piece. It's a bit of history that they refuse to even gawk at. And that's not just family. There are some friends of family who have looked at it and had the same reaction, but react in no way at all when they see a hammer and sickle on the spines of other volumes. What the huh?

The people of this country are so thoroughly indoctrinated into a society that no longer grimaces at the symbols of the Red Menace, that they don't even think of the Soviets as an evil empire anymore, but rather as more victims of "American Imperialism." When asked to name monstrous or racist writers a bare handful will pull out Hitler or his ilk, while the rest will shout out Jefferson or Washington. Our history has been demonized, but not just ours. Any history that feels uncomfortable to people is being either brushed aside, or labeled as destructive, regardless of how instructive and important it is. Another friend, seeing me reading this same book, after remarking that it's important to know this history, so as not to repeat it, then commented that he hoped we weren't headed there right now, meaning he equated Trump with Hitler. An otherwise intelligent man, brainwashed by so much propaganda from the Left-owned media elite that he was spouting off sound bites without even realizing it. Yet another friend, in a more realistic mindset, in talking about the next presidential election confided to me, "Doesn't matter who wins. F*ck 'em: my powder's dry."

Know your history, people. Find out why people are doing the things that they are doing; why they've been doing them this way for a long time; and why they will continue to do them until the last two of us are hitting each other with stones (dying last makes you the winner, dontchaknow?)

The enemy already thinks you're racist, sexist, transphobe, Islamaphobe, what-the-hell-ever-phobe. Their opinions are worthless, groundless, and not worth your time or effort to suss out. Live your life as you see fit, and to hell with it offending anyone else, just so long as how you see fit doesn't stop them from living how they see fit. Don't go along to get along, but dig in like a tick to your own moral code, and be prepared to die rather than do something dishonorable. In short: be a good guy. At least then you'll die with a clean heart.

<u>**Showers of Optimism**</u>
(The Libertarian Enterprise Nov. 17, 2019)

Let's inject a bit of optimism, shall we?

Y'see, it occurs to me that in so many places the takeaway from news is that we're all doomed. Politically, financially, environmentally, we're so hosed that it just isn't worth the effort any more. This has led to countless impressionable younger folks swearing off having babies, or just swearing off life. The endless doomsday propaganda forced into the heads of those younger and more inexperienced than us old farts has all but created a generation of manic depressives who look at a brilliant new morning and see nothing but the oncoming storm. They opt to check out because those that mold them have told them that no matter what they do they're screwed, so in truth, who can blame them?

Nihilism is an emotional ideology that sickens me. But, you know what: if you want to be the kind of prick who believes in nothing but the futility of it all, you go right ahead, and kick your can all the way into oblivion, you oven-heated putz. But don't start spreading your vile anti-creed to the kids who aren't yet aware enough of the glories of life to see your shit for what it is. Screw you. Keep it to yourself, and let them mess their lives up in their own way. Mush mouthed, self-righteous, triggered bastards.

What I can see from just a cursory glimpse of the propaganda machine that falsely promotes itself as news is a whole faction of the populace that'd rather let it burn than be wrong about something. They will do whatever they can to remove a sitting President because he's f*cked up their elitist status quo. God help us if anyone ever takes a successful pop at the Donald. There'd be blood in the streets.

Because that selfsame faction of the populace would take to the streets shouting and cheering like it was the day the Berlin Wall fell, and the remaining, infinitely more sane, population of this greatest country in the world will see red. Hand to God I hope this never happens, but they're trying so hard to make it so that I wonder how far optimism has to stretch before it becomes delusion.

Contrary to (supposedly) overwhelming popular opinion, I feel that things are going just fine. After eight years under the racist, anti-American yolk of Saint Barry, there'd have to be a pretty dark drop to make me see things as anything other than better. My family is in good shape, as are my friends, and the vast majority of folks that I know. Interestingly enough the only folks that I know that are having a hard time of it are the ones who got fat suckling off the government teat under Barry, and who are now looking at a world where they potentially have to— gasp!—take care of their own shit. Welcome to the human race, pal. Get a helmet or get off the field. It's called life: live it.

Things are better. The country is becoming more financial solid every day. Our troops are being slowly removed from foreign conflicts that we never should have gotten involved in in the first place. The Communists (I refuse to call them Democrats any more: there can be no doubt in even the thickest head just where their political loyalties lie) are losing their minds more every time one of them talks. Yep: getting better.

See, for a long time I was worried about just what kind of future we were barreling into. For years I was certain that we were actively entering Philip K. Dick's bleak tomorrow with no chance to pull back from the cliff. I'd hoped for Heinlein's, but we as a species just aren't that good, I fear. Still, what I see now might not be a golden utopia of Constitutional freedom, but it isn't necessarily going to be a fascist wet dream either. For the first time in a long time I find myself thinking like Sara Conner at the end of the last (good) Terminator movie. I'm not sure where we're headed.

As a youth, and well into my whiny 20's, I was a solid pessimist. I just figured we'd do each other in, that sooner or later the comet would win, and that I'd be lucky to see 35. I'm looking down 40's tailpipe now, and see a bit of silver lining. 'Bout a decade back, my incredible wife and I ushered the first of two perfect girls into the world. They give me as much hope for the future as anything else. Though it's not for them that I find myself being bright and shiny. They help, don't get me wrong, but I find that my whole outlook has shifted from shitty browns to brilliant light.

See, we've survived this far. We've made it through the population boom that was supposed to have us all starving and cannibalistic and living on top of each other a few decades back. We made it through the supposedly inevitable nuclear war with the soviets that'd have each of us roasting at ground zero. We've made it through more than a decade of "Seven more years" environmentalist doom and gloom porno, and I suspect that we'll make it through seventy more. Because there's more of us looking at the incompetent powers that shouldn't be and saying, "Y'know what: you're full of it." The wool might not have been pulled from the eyes of all of us, but there's enough of us who see them for the crap mongers that they are to shake their unearned power center to its core.

So, again: things are getting better. Overpopulation, nuclear war, global warming, and Commie incompetence haven't done us in yet, and I don't figure they will. Because we're Americans, and even after more than 200 years that still stands for something. Grit, God-willing, and a refusal to stay down. We don't roll over for monsters, and when the fight comes we finish it. So, even if there's a couple of bad years ahead as the lamenters of the late USSR do their best to instill in us their amoral, anti-human garbage ideologies before finally (and much belatedly) shuffling off this mortal coil, we'll come through it ok. It's what we do, and they just can't help but hate that.

That all being said, I'll just close with some advice. Keep it together folks. Look at the bright side. Wrong is wrong, no matter how many bastards cry at you that it's right. You owe no one anything by proxy. We're doing just fine. Keep living your life right, if for no other reason than because it just irks the bastards. No matter how grumpy you are, someone loves you: so be worth it. 'Bout sums it up.

Have a better one.

<u>New History</u>
(*The Libertarian Enterprise Dec. 1, 2019*)

Going to make a bit of a prediction. Honestly I'm not sure where this little rant is going to go, so please bare with me. I'll get there… I think.

So…

A lot has been written about the current cancel culture, and to say that those who'd just assume erase anything and everything that they find offensive are unstable is to say that water's wet. It's beyond obvious. Everything bothers these snowflakes. And, not to sound too paranoid, but I can see the reasoning behind this as nothing short of destroying the legacy that is America.

Y'see, they've got no problem with touting the supposed greatness and achievements of the lamented former USSR, or any of its Red, individuality- and freedom hating cohorts, but are at the front of every line of hive-minded spaghetti-spines when it comes to demonizing each and every action of any person who ever lived in this, the home of the brave. Beating a dead horse here, but it's worth repeating, so let me repeat it: They hate us.

They hate everything we've done, as a culture. Now, don't get me wrong: we're hardly snow white, but neither are we the great Satan. People are in better condition in the United States today, even in the lowest of the lower income areas of every city, than they are in any socialist haven, and if there's a single doubt as to the validity of that statement then you should just look to see how the other half lives.

What they hate is that we've made it work. The whole American Dream. The ascendence of the individual. The achievement of the single person, over the collective. For each and every man and woman in this country who goes out and makes something of themselves, in spite of the odds and the perceived belief of leftists everywhere that we can do nothing apart from the whole, their whole worldview is shown for the hollow, humanity-hating, dictatorial, iron fisted thing that it is. We are a testament to greatness, but not the testament that they need us to be.

This is nothing new, though, and I worry that it's not even temporal, which is where my bit of a prediction comes in.

Earlier today I saw an article proclaiming that a certain Evil politician is attempting to push through a bill that would posthumously strip Metal of Honor winners of their Metals of Honor, many, many years after the fact. A few months ago (maybe years; not sure) I'd written that anyone historical who was held up to the modern left's ideas of civility would fall well short. I'd written that it was not only foolish but downright stupid to hold anyone before us up to the light of endless discrimination that permeates contemporary society. Here we see why. People dead for decades or centuries, lampooned if not outright demonized, without ability to defend themselves, for no other reason than to be low hanging fruit for someone less worthy.

But it doesn't stop there. It can't. It feels to me that all of this is but a stepping stone to what they're trying to get. Namely: Posthumous Impeachment.

Sounds crazy and paranoid, I know, but let me meander about this for a moment.

The founding fathers have been promoted for at least the last two decades as monsters, racists, and slave-owners. Pieces of garbage that are not only unworthy of our notice, but deserving of our outright hatred. Unless we're talking about Hamilton, though the less said about that man the better. Washington and Jefferson, in particular, have been targeted by Democratic politicians and revisionist historians specifically. Why? Because Washington set the standard, and damn few have lived up to it. And Jefferson was an individualist and promoter of limited government. You remove them, take away the Godhead stature associated with them, and the whole foundation that our republic is built on starts to crumble.

For the Socialist narrative to progress, these folks have to go. If beastly politician lady gets her bill pushed through (and who wouldn't want it pushed through with all good haste, unless they're racist old white men anyway, right?), her sights will broaden, and in time we'll be looking at those posthumous impeachments, where folks like Washington and Jefferson, but also any and every right-leaning promoter of individual liberty, will be scrubbed from memory, seen as nothing more than unfortunate stains on the pages of proper, Socialized history.

So, people, here's my recommendation for the week: go out to used book stores and pick up as many volumes of American history as you can get your grubby little hands on, and horde them. Yes, I know, digital takes up less room, but it's also more susceptible to revision. That paperbound, dead tree edition that you have in a box in your attic, though? It is what it is, and Big Brother can't do anything about it without your knowing. So hold onto them like the precious jewels that they are. Because it won't be long until that history that you've always known, that you've always taken for granted, won't be available anymore. After that? It may as well not have happened at all.

<u>Rocking the Big Red Boat</u>
(The Libertarian Enterprise Dec 8, 2019)

No matter how often they fail, the Socialists keep coming back, telling us that this time it'll be different.   This time we'll get it right, if only the capitalists will not stop the train of progress.   This time all of the hard learned lessons will be taken into account, and a new golden age will finally, at long last, be upon us. This time, this time…

To paraphrase Niven, reality trumps theory every time. And though he was talking about speeds in Einstein space, the idea is solid nevertheless, and easily transferable to everyday life. In this case: the theory of Socialism, with its plentiful bounty and a good life to be had by all, is swept away by the harsh realities of the twentieth century, which left millions dead and countless others so beaten down and subject to dictatorial whim as to be essentially little more than wandering skin bags.

Through the actions of those in charge, and the inaction of those who didn't want to rock the Big Red Boat, we've made a generation of permanent cripples and parasites, who see work and individual achievement as synonymous with evil.   Folks who are so latched onto the government teat that to ever set off under their own steam is so terrifying an idea that should they be faced with it they'd shrivel up and die. This safety net society is killing us, and leading not down a road to a brighter tomorrow, but is rather backtracking into a yesterday that is already overflowing in blood.

There's no teaching some folks.   They can look at each and every stumble and fall and say, "Not me.   I'll never make that kind of mistake.   I'll get it right the first time, gee, aren't I just the best?"

Then there's us other folks. The ones who know better. The ones with a sense of history, who see the bloodbaths behind us and before us and know that nothing good can ever come from this because the starting premise is flawed. Theft is theft, no matter how you polish it up. To punish some for achieving while rewarding others for lowering the status quo does nothing but give the achievers no incentive to achieve and the parasites no will to better themselves. In short: Socialism is EVIL.

Though I can still look at the future with hope —I am a science fiction reader after all, and at its best that's the genre of optimism—there are days when I want to beg folks to shut it all down. Let me be clear: I am in no way promoting suicide or property damage or anything of the sort. I have a moral opposition to the taking of one's own life, and to destroy private property is something altogether sickening to me, and is nothing short of an assault on the person of that property's owner. No, I'm asking if it's isn't time for the achievers to say to hell with it and walk off. Take what they've earned and let society drop down into the dark age that Socialist Democrats are begging for.

But, I digress.

I've started this last paragraph a couple times now, and keep getting sidetracked by meandering thoughts. Should I mention Rand, I wonder, her work being heavily in my mind of late? Do I bring it around to the Democrats and their increasing insanity? Do I mention the fella who tried to make me feel like an idiot for saying how happy it makes me feel to see one of these monsters fall flat on their faces? No. What I'll do, what I find myself doing more often anymore (comes from being a dad, I guess), is to offer some advice. Keep rocking the boat. Don't knuckle under, no matter the pressure. Don't give up. Give the ones that come after us something worth inheriting, not a forever war to keep those freedoms given to us by God. In short: be heroes.

<u>Dear Future Americans</u>
(*The Libertarian Enterprise Jan. 12, 2020*)

Dear future Americans,

You don't know me, but given my two children, and how many young'uns they're likely to have, and so on and so on, down through the generations, it's just as likely that if you're reading this a hundred generations on as not that I'm one of your progenitors. So, for the sake of clarity, and to tweak my own already inflated sense of worth, you can call me Gran'pa Harry. You can probably thank me for the gray hair and I'd like to take some credit for your general disdain toward authority in all of its forms. For your smarts, good looks, and incredible grit you can thank your 100-generations removed grandmother. She's a peach.

I'm writing to you today (January 1, 2020) to give you a perspective on your ancestors, so that you might know us better. See, I'm not sure how the history books will portray those of us that look at statism and socialism as an unnecessary Evil; Who roll our eyes at attempts to politically correct every aspect of life and history; Who keep out steel sharp and out powder dry, waiting until the Left takes things just one step too far. In all likelihood, we'll be shown in a bad light, much as we are being shown now. We'll all be looked at as antisocial, or racist, or sexist, or whatever are the bad guy tag lines of your time. So let me start off there: it just isn't so.

Given the amount of folks that I have to interact with, through my job, and church functions, etc., I have the opportunity to know people of many walks of life, with as diverse a mix of social and political opinions as you're likely to come by. And I can say, by and large, that there's very few bigots in the lot of them. The people that are being violently maligned today are the ones who are in fact less bigoted, as they insist on (gasp!) holding all people, regardless of gender, race, or religion, to the same standards, giving preference to none. We're hated, in fact, because we won't turn a blind eye, regardless of who you are, but will hold everybody accountable, consequences be damned.

And make no mistake: there are consequences. We're abused, both verbally and physically, by the same folks who say that we're the violent, vulgar ones. We're called fascists because we hold the Bill of Rights up as the highest law of the land. We're accused of discrimination because we don't go in for coveting what our neighbor's got, and don't want that neighbor to covet what we've earned. We're labeled antisocial because we just want to be left alone, to live our lives as we see fit, bending knee only to God and the woman we want to marry. In short: they hate us because we're a constant, savage reminder of just what an American is meant to be.

Ironically, as a group, we read lots of westerns, histories, and science fiction. Maybe it's because we like to know where we've been, and enjoy speculating about where we're going. It's where we are right now that's failed us. You see, for the better part of a century, at least as far back as FRD, we've been under siege, our livelihoods and individual freedoms (which have been rightly referred to as "God-given rights") assaulted by people who can only be referred to as the enemy. Let me tell you a bit about them.

The liberal political establishment, regardless of whatever name they emerge under—democrat, democratic socialist, communist, what have you—is completely opposed to the American way of life. By any definition, they're insane. They look at every example of their political ideology that 20th century history has to offer, and ignore the blood of millions. They see a failed experiment in communal living by force, and tell themselves that this time it will work. Just like every one of their predecessors said to themselves. And with the same inevitable result. The history of the last century is a tally of blood, drained from all of us, in the name of "Progress."

One of the lessons that the left-leaning clusters of the world never seem to learn is that forced equality isn't equality. They promote the idea of making everyone rich by stripping the already rich of their money and property, and the economically downtrodden, who've been told for their entire lives that it's not their fault they're poor, it's the wealthy that are doing it, hear it and jump at the chance. The same economically downtrodden who have been left behind by every single government works project, and welfare scheme, willingly become the foot soldiers of the lunatic powers that be. Millions die, in the name of some idealized equality whereby all are equal, at last, though in such a wretched state that they'd have been better off just leaving things as they were. This is the lesson that honest socialist history teaches us. Never forger it. And never forget that the people that promote this way of life, this monstrosity of a political ideology that has led to the deaths of millions in each and every case, are murderers. If not in fact then by proxy. And no matter who you are, they're always going to be gunning for you.

-Aside: "Gunning for you" is a perfect, if ironic, choice of phrases, when it comes to these folks, who are perpetually doing their best to disarm the general populace. Make no mistake, my intelligent descendants: the only reason an authority wants to take away your means of fighting back is so that you can't defend yourself against them. They fear you. They know what you can do, and it terrifies them. So hold on to your hardware with both hands, and be ready to fight to keep it. But, I digress-

I'm not sure what kind of a world you're living in right now. If all goes well, you're going to be living on many worlds, seeking out your living by the sweat of your brow, and not stealing it from those who can. I hope that this is the case. I feel a reason for my current optimism is the blatantly obvious fact that the modern left are losing their minds. Never stable in the first place, they were at least able to hide most of their lunacy/stupidity behind a smile that was nothing more than a shining turd. Nowadays, as their every step is getting either tripped or downright blown back, they're losing even that fingertip grip on reality that's kept them out of padded rooms for most of their lives. They're showing the world just how unstable they are. And society is at long last standing up to them and saying, "No more."

There are many here and now who think that a war is coming. I can't help but think that it is already here, and has been for a very long time. It's the oldest conflict, a perpetual stalemate between light and darkness, between advancement and an everlasting dark age. And though it may prove me more fanciful than I see myself, it does appear that light is winning.

I write. I mean, obviously. I try to write science fiction, though find that I'm not smart enough to pull it off. As such, I smilingly call my scribbles space opera or science fantasy. In truth, that still might be seen as delusions of grandeur. Though as I've said before: of what use are delusions of mediocrity?   In much the same spirit, I believe that whatever future you find yourselves in is a good one. One in which the light has won, and the stagnant armies of darkness are at long last beaten back into the nothing that they've always been.   I believe that you're saved.

So, I will end this by wishing you all well, but also to remind you that things are worth fighting for, and we are fighting; that you should know your history, or else become history yourselves; that the price of your continued freedoms is your eternal vigilance.   Never forget that you're not only the legacy of those that came before, but are also the heroes or villains of those that will follow.   You may never set out to be a role model, but you will be to someone. So: be worth it.

Sincerely,
Gran'pa Harry

<u>**A Review of the *Fleet of Worlds* Series by Niven and Lerner**</u>
(*The Libertarian Enterprise Feb. 16, 2020*)

So, let's talk about Larry Niven.

I think I was about thirteen when my uncle gave me a paperback copy of Niven and Pournelle's *Footfall.* It was the first thing that I'd read by either man. For about a month I struggled through the first 80 or so pages, feeling like it was just beyond me, and was about ready to give up, when all of a sudden the Fithp hit with a vengeance. The remainder of the book was devoured over a long, sleepless night. Since then, I've read it a couple of times, and as I get older (though not necessarily smarter) I've come to enjoy those hard first 80 pages as much as the rest of the book. World building, man.

Over these intervening years I've gone on to read everything that these two men—along with Steven Barnes and Michael Flynn—have written together, and although I admit to finding *The Gripping Hand* to be the least of their works, have never been outright let down by their words. It seems to me that with most co-written books (though not all) the default mode for so many creators is to unintentionally showcase what their faults are rather than their strengths.   There are some obvious exceptions to this, however: Smith and Zelman come to mind. The greatest exception to the rule, however, for me anyway, is Niven and Pournelle, who although they wrote some great stuff individually, were never better than when they were working together. Though each did indeed do many books, short stories, etc. solo.

Which, in a roundabout way, leads us to *Ringworld.*

Niven's *Ringworld* is an award-winning classic of science fiction, and filled with so many large concepts that when reading it the first time my eyes must have been bugging out. Set firmly in his Known Space series, it works as a kind of epic culmination of everything that he'd been writing about for years. By the end of the initial four book series, he'd managed to tie together most, if not all, of his related KS stories into a coherent whole, driving the narrative with such a fierce push that readers were left breathless, even through scenes where nothing more exciting happened than four characters riding sky bikes around looking at things for 30 pages.

It's been years since I last read any of the Ringworld books other than that first, and in truth, lots of the fine details of books 2-4 have left my increasingly addled memory, leaving only the bigger swaths of narrative behind. But I've had some very fond reminiscences of the stories, even the ones that I felt were too cleaver by far. So when, a few months back, trolling the stacks of my local library looking for some new and interesting science fiction my eyes crossed over a copy of *Fleet of Worlds* by Mr. Niven and Edward M. Lerner, I got a mad case of the "Gosh-wow"'s and picked it up.

For anyone who doesn't know, *Fleet of worlds* is the first of a four (or five) book series, each one building on the breadcrumbs of the others, until the story becomes large enough to encompass the whole of Niven's Known Space. The first book gives you a more inside look at the social and personal lives of the Puppeteers, one of the forefront alien species of the KS series, while letting the reader get up close and person with Nessus, one of the main characters from the first *Ringworld* book and others. It's a solid read, full of interesting characters, action, and mind puzzles that made me look forward to reading it each time I sat down to do so. While it gives interesting background on a lot of subjects, it's written in a smooth enough way, with nearly no reliance of previous works to make it work, that you could use it as your first excursion into Niven's worlds and you wouldn't feel left out in the breeze.

The second book *Juggler of Worlds,* however, cannot claim to be so easy to get into. Don't get me wrong, it's an absolutely wonderful book, but relies so heavily on parts of a previous KS collection, *Crashlander,* and the short story "The Soft Weapon," that there are whole narrative threads left hanging as they'd already been completed elsewhere. If you're new to the universe, then this will frustrate you to no end. If, however, you're already a fan, and have got through *Crashlander* and "The Soft Weapon," then this books pays out in spades, as it gives you a real secret history kind of vibe, adding to the depth of an already deep and complex universe.

With *Destroyer of Worlds,* things start to come to a head, with the reintroduction of a race of beasties first introduced in Niven's *Protector,* giving the series, which until now had relied mostly on politics and interpersonal relationships to provide its antagonism, a solid set of villains to deal with. The Pak are interesting characters themselves, though rarely seen bodily in the book except through the main characters interactions with one of their race. Without spoiling too much, there's incoming alien armadas, intent of genocide of everything, worlds getting blows to bits that could have been written by one of the great world destroyer writers of the golden age, and a climax that just sings.

The final book of the four prologues to *Ringworld, Betrayer of Worlds,* does a very solid job of pulling together all of the narrative threads of the first three books, and not only gives us an ending worth reading, but sets up *Ringworld* itself very nicely. After completing *Betrayer* I reread *Ringworld* for the first time in years, and was astounded at just how many things the *Fleet* adds to the original novel. Not only are we given a solid, more sympathetic look into the workings of Nessus, we're also shown Wu in his earlier years. So many things that are glossed over in *Ringworld* are elaborated on in this last book that it was like reading it again for the first time.

I know that given time I'm going to have to go through *Engineers, Throne,* and *Children,* the other three *Ringworld* books, if only to have the full picture before jumping into *Fate of Worlds,* the fifth and final of Niven and Lerner's novels. I look forward to this. I've written more often than I should that there are so few writers alive that I read, that to say these two folks are on that list is a lot. Over about a month I read over a thousand pages of this story, and never for a moment had a regret. Too many times I get to the end of a book, and lament the time wasted, that could have been better served reading something better. I cannot say that about these books. They were good, intelligent, and entertaining. Five stars all around.

Unpaid Debts…

God, without whom nothing is possible, and through whom nothing is impossible. My incredible, long-suffering wife, Naomi, indispensable in every way. Our daughters, who can bring light and joy to any situation, and who make their parents prouder every day. Ken Holder, L. Neil Smith, and the whole crew of delightful rabble-rousers at TLE, for not only making the best 'zine on the web, but also proving to a younger me that I wasn't alone in my wish for freedom and to be just left alone. The many folks that I've never met in person (with one exception), but who nevertheless went above and beyond to be helpful and just plain cool. Robert A. Heinlein, H. Beam Piper, Dean Koontz, and many other artists and creators who I was enough of a mind with as to not lament giving them my money. And you, dear reader, who gave over your earned cash, and dedicated your precious time, to reading this short collection of rants. I hope you liked it.

H.G.M